# The Good News About Global Poverty

## What Americans Believe About the World's Poor— and What Churches Can Do to Help

Research commissioned by
Compassion International,
Colorado Springs, Colorado

Research conducted by
Barna Group, Ventura, California

Funding for this research was made possible by the generous support of Compassion International. Barna Group was solely responsible for data collection, analysis and writing of the report.

# TABLE OF CONTENTS

# CONCLUSION

# APPENDIX

# INTRODUCTION

Dear pastor,

Compassion International commissioned this research project with the Barna Group to provide you with a tool that reveals the U.S. Church's views toward global poverty. We are excited to place this resource in your hands and pray it will be valuable in your efforts to develop disciples who deeply engage in caring for the poor.

At Compassion, we are enthusiasts for and servants to the local church. Throughout our 65 years of ministry, we have frequently witnessed firsthand how the Church brings hope and life in Jesus' name to the "least of these." We believe that Jesus and his Church are and always will be God's "Plan A" to reveal his love to a world that desperately needs it.

Jesus and his teachings are at the very heart of our ministry—our mission statement is simply "Releasing children from poverty in Jesus' name." It is his example of considering the poor and oppressed that compels us forward. The Greek word *splagchnizomai* was used to refer to Jesus' compassion. It describes more than just an emotion; it also depicts action, a deep stirring in your core that moves you to do something because you can't sit idly by while the innocent suffer.

This action-based understanding of Jesus' compassion is what fuels our desire to release children from poverty in his name. Recent research has shown that there are 385 million children living in extreme poverty, as defined as living on less than a $1.90 a day.[1] But even that staggering proportion is nothing compared to the number of Jesus followers in the world today. It's powerful to think that their generosity alone could alleviate the suffering of every child currently being ravaged by extreme poverty.

While the magnitude of millions of children living in poverty can easily feel overwhelming, the truth is that each one is a precious individual in the eyes of Jesus. That's why, following Jesus' mandate to disciple individuals, Compassion has chosen holistic discipleship as our model for life

**SANTIAGO "JIMMY" MELLADO**

President and CEO
Compassion International

## ABOUT THE RESEARCH

Barna Group has conducted multiple studies in partnership with Compassion International for more than 25 years, and much of that historic data is represented comparatively throughout this report. This particular study included two online quantitative surveys conducted in May 2017, one among 1,001 U.S. adults and another among 609 U.S. Protestant senior pastors. For full details about this and other studies covered in this report, please refer to the Methodology in the Appendix.

transformation with each child entrusted to us. In partnership with local churches, both in the U.S. and around the world, children in our program receive spiritual, economic, social and physical care to help them transcend what is often a multi-generational cycle of poverty.

Having personally served churches for over 25 years in my ministry calling, I have loved seeing the potential of pastors like you to bring change in this world. As you will see in the research contained in *The Good News About Global Poverty,* yours is the most significant voice that can inspire the Church to be a powerful force in eradicating poverty. I pray you will be moved with compassion and inspired to even greater action as you review the findings, infographics and interviews in the following pages.

May God bless this resource to support you and your church well as you care for the global poor in Jesus' name. Thank you for allowing us to journey with you in this precious cause.

In Christ,

Santiago "Jimmy" Mellado

# VIEW ONLINE

Watch an exclusive conversation between Jimmy Mellado, CEO of Compassion International, and David Kinnaman, President of Barna, as they discuss some of the recent findings from our research partnership and how churches and individuals are joining together to help end global poverty.

Watch a video from Barna Studios about perspectives of global poverty and the hope for eradicating it in this generation.

To view videos and gain additional insights on this research, please visit
www.barna.com/goodnewsaboutglobalpoverty

# AT A GLANCE

**1**

Global poverty is on the decline, though the American public is generally unaware of this fact.

70 percent incorrectly assume international poverty has increased, even though millions have been lifted out of poverty in the past 25 years.

**2**

People feel an urgency about the issue of poverty—especially those in the Church.

One-quarter of all U.S. adults (24%) and a third of practicing Christians (34%) are "extremely" concerned about international poverty.

**3**

Four in 10 adults (39%) assign the primary responsibility of addressing global poverty to governments.

The political climate and ideologies of U.S. adults, however, permeate and sometimes complicate reactions to poverty.

**4**

24 percent of Americans prioritize personal action to expand access to education.

Other initiatives that help children, like anti-trafficking efforts, child evangelism and orphan care, also rank highly for pastors and Christians.

**5**

People esteem church leaders as authorities on poverty

54 percent of practicing Christians and 39 percent of adults "definitely" trust faith leaders on the subject.

**6**

## ... even though pastors need to be convinced of their potential impact.

Fewer pastors today than in 2008 believe one person can make a difference, and just one-third (32%) thinks ending poverty is "doable."

**7**

## More than a third of pastors (34%) sees spiritual health as the key to poverty alleviation.

They also emphasize causes like church-building overseas, and one in four (24%) considers the involvement of U.S. churches to be critical.

**8**

## Anti-poverty activism is often led from the margins.

Ethnic minorities are more inspired about ending poverty and are more apt than white Americans to give charitably.

**9**

## Action against poverty is concentrated among a compassionate, highly engaged segment.

Donors to global poverty care about a range of social issues and volunteer more for churches and non-profits.

**10**

## Optimism about poverty or personal influence connects to greater involvement.

57 percent of U.S. adults say they would do even more if they knew they could make a difference.

# A QUARTER OF A CENTURY IN GLOBAL POVERTY

An overview of poverty levels and perceptions since 1990

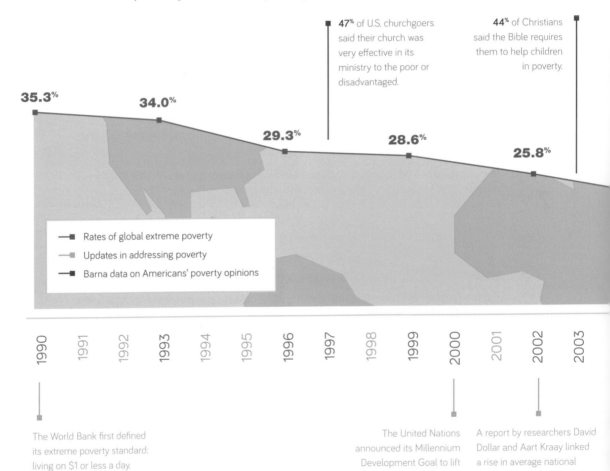

**47%** of U.S. churchgoers said their church was very effective in its ministry to the poor or disadvantaged.

**44%** of Christians said the Bible requires them to help children in poverty.

35.3%  34.0%  29.3%  28.6%  25.8%

- Rates of global extreme poverty
- Updates in addressing poverty
- Barna data on Americans' poverty opinions

1990  1991  1992  1993  1994  1995  1996  1997  1998  1999  2000  2001  2002  2003

The World Bank first defined its extreme poverty standard: living on $1 or less a day.

The United Nations announced its Millennium Development Goal to lift 1 billion people out of poverty by 2015—which was met by 2010.

A report by researchers David Dollar and Aart Kraay linked a rise in average national incomes—such as in growing nations like China, India and Brazil—with a decrease in extreme poverty.

August 1997, n=1,003 U.S. adults who attend a Christian church; May 2003, n=1,002, U.S. adults; June 2008, n=494 U.S. senior pastors; September 2011, n=1,429 U.S. adults; December 2013, n=1,052 U.S. adults; May 2017, n=1,001 U.S. adults, 609 U.S. senior pastors.

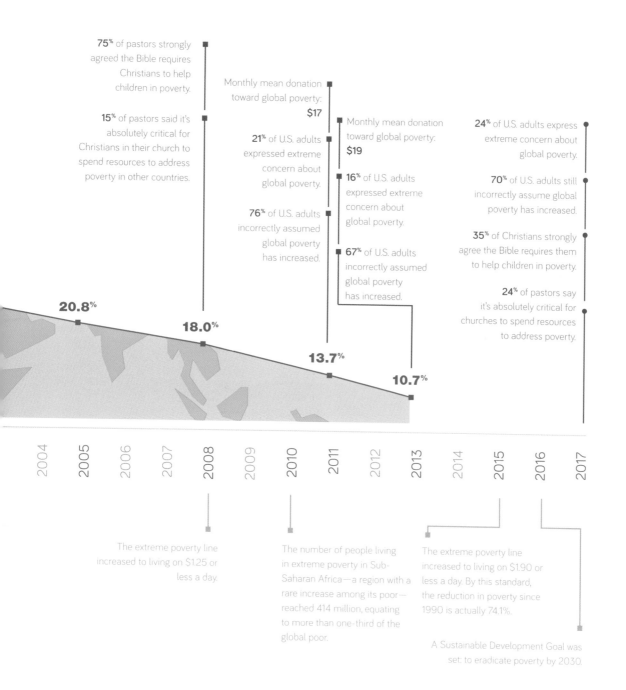

**75%** of pastors strongly agreed the Bible requires Christians to help children in poverty.

**15%** of pastors said it's absolutely critical for Christians in their church to spend resources to address poverty in other countries.

Monthly mean donation toward global poverty: **$17**

**21%** of U.S. adults expressed extreme concern about global poverty.

**76%** of U.S. adults incorrectly assumed global poverty has increased.

Monthly mean donation toward global poverty: **$19**

**16%** of U.S. adults expressed extreme concern about global poverty.

**67%** of U.S. adults incorrectly assumed global poverty has increased.

**24%** of U.S. adults express extreme concern about global poverty.

**70%** of U.S. adults still incorrectly assume global poverty has increased.

**35%** of Christians strongly agree the Bible requires them to help children in poverty.

**24%** of pastors say it's absolutely critical for churches to spend resources to address poverty.

**20.8%**  **18.0%**  **13.7%**  **10.7%**

2004  2005  2006  2007  2008  2009  2010  2011  2012  2013  2014  2015  2016  2017

The extreme poverty line increased to living on $1.25 or less a day.

The number of people living in extreme poverty in Sub-Saharan Africa—a region with a rare increase among its poor—reached 414 million, equating to more than one-third of the global poor.

The extreme poverty line increased to living on $1.90 or less a day. By this standard, the reduction in poverty since 1990 is actually 74.1%.

A Sustainable Development Goal was set: to eradicate poverty by 2030.

Sources: https://data.worldbank.org/topic/poverty?end=2014&start=1990 •
http://www.politifact.com/global-news/statements/2016/mar/23/gayle-smith/did-we-really-reduce-extreme-poverty-half-30-years/ •
https://ourworldindata.org/extreme-poverty/#poverty-traps • https://www.un.org/millenniumgoals/pdf/report-2013/mdg-report-2013-english.pdf

# PERCEPTIONS OF POVERTY

1

## A SUMMARY OF AMERICAN OPINIONS ABOUT THE WORLD'S POOR

Poverty, in the most basic terms, refers to not having enough. But beyond that simple definition, the meaning and reality of poverty become very complicated—not to mention that the criterion of "enough" depends on one's context and can vary by age, climate, health and local economy.

The World Bank has created one measure, based on the cost of goods necessary for people to survive, that can be applied broadly to global material poverty. That international extreme poverty line is $1.90 a day (about $700 a year) or less.[2] According to this international poverty standard, there is good news: a drop of 200 million people living in poverty between 2012 and 2015. The bigger picture is also encouraging: in 1990, the world poverty rate was 35 percent. Since then, 1.1 billion people have been lifted out of poverty.[3]

Of course, that still leaves an estimated 700 million people—11 percent of the world's current population—living in extreme poverty.[4] Half of the people in extreme poverty live in Sub-Saharan Africa, 13.5 percent in South Asia and 12 percent live in East Asia. Sub-Saharan Africa's poverty levels are declining slower than the rest of the world's; many countries in this region have poverty rates well over 50 percent. In Zimbabwe, for example, the rate of people living in poverty is as high as 72 percent.[5]

Rates are typically high in areas of conflict, such as Afghanistan (36%), Pakistan (30%) and Iraq (23%), where the effects of poverty are brutal and ever-present.[6] Diseases like polio which have been stamped out in wealthier countries continue to take away lives and the ability to work in Pakistan, Nigeria and Afghanistan.[7] Poisonous air pollutants, such as ammonia, are concentrated in cities with poorer populations, such as Lagos, Nigeria; Delhi, India; and Bangkok, Thailand.[8] The countries whose citizens witness the highest levels of corruption also tend to be among the world's poorest, led by Somalia, South Sudan, North Korea and Syria.[9]

Ultimately, these percentages and definitions can never tell the full story of poverty, one that entraps individuals around the world and manifests not only in financial scarcity, but exploitation, illness and isolation. Extreme poverty, by global standards, is also something very few American adults experience or even encounter, certainly not frequently enough to have perspective on its life cycle.

Yet, when using these widely accepted barometers for the severity of poverty, there *is* notable progress to report: The global trend is one of less and less extreme poverty. This report's title—*The Good News About Global Poverty*—refers chiefly to this fact, as well as the demonstrated power of compassion and optimism in addressing poverty and the U.S. Church's role in facilitating justice for the poor, a principal component of the "good news" all Christians are called to share. If the recorded decline in worldwide poverty is not yet cause for celebration, it's at least reason to hope and—following the lead of the Church in the developing world—incentive to continue chipping away at poverty and its effects. Backed by decades of verifiable improvement, now is not a time for complacency, but for building momentum and elucidating effective methods.

First, however, Americans might need a crash course on the facts about poverty.

## WHAT PEOPLE DON'T KNOW ABOUT POVERTY (YET)

When Barna polled U.S. adults to see if they believe poverty is growing, shrinking or holding steady, it became clear that public understanding has not kept up with the gradual reduction in global poverty. Overall, people are unaware of the positive direction in which poverty has moved over the last 25 years. Although extreme global poverty has fallen by 24 percentage points since 1990, most U.S. adults (70%) believe it has *increased*.

This misconception is still a bit less bleak than it was in the past. The percentage of adults who gave an answer in line with the World Bank's encouraging report increased by 6 points, to 13 percent, since a 2011 study.

Americans—especially younger ones—feel urgency surrounding poverty; nine out of 10 (91%) are troubled when reminded of the great number of people who do not have access to clean water, sufficient food, clothing, shelter or basic medicine. One-fourth (24%) selects an "extreme" level of concern for the global poor, even in light of the many pressing issues facing Americans

Public understanding has not kept up with the gradual reduction in global poverty today. (In the next chapter, we'll delve into the sincerity and practical application of this sentiment.)

## "Since 1990, Global Poverty Has …"

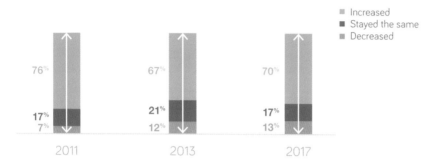

2011, *n*=993 U.S. adults; 2013, *n*=1,025 U.S. adults; May 2017, *n*=1,001 U.S. adults.

## Level of Concern Regarding Global Poverty

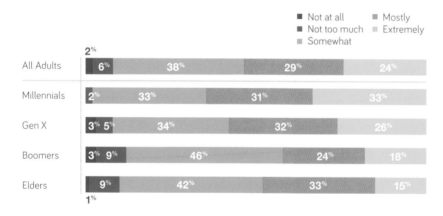

May 2017, *n*=1,001 U.S. adults.

## Despite Lack of Knowledge, Christians Express Deep Concern

Compared to the general population, Christians, including practicing ones, are similarly oblivious that international poverty is improving. Those who meet Barna's definition of "evangelical" (see glossary in the Appendix for

## Practicing Christians' Concern for Extreme Global Poverty

■ Not at all    ■ Mostly
■ Not too much  ■ Extremely
■ Somewhat

2011, n=274 practicing Christians; 2013, n=249 practicing Christians; May 2017, n=219 practicing Christians.

Among practicing Christians today, reported concern for extreme global poverty holds strong

details) are the least likely group (9%) to say they already knew about a 25-year reduction in global poverty—though it's possible they are merely the group most likely to *admit* being unaware!

Regardless of their understanding of the current global poverty levels, the faithful consistently report a concern for it. After all, they've had good teachers: As long as there has been a Church, addressing poverty has been a focus of its texts and its programs. Some monastic orders, the U.S. School Lunch Program, individuals like George Mueller or Mother Teresa and the multifaceted efforts of faith-based, non-governmental organizations are just some of the relatively recent testaments to this religiously motivated generosity. Among practicing Christians today, reported concern for extreme global poverty holds strong. The vast majority (94%) is at least somewhat concerned, one-third "extremely" so (34%), consistent with percentages in 2011.

This sensitivity is permeated by positivity, as practicing Christians are relatively hopeful about their ability to affect poverty. A majority feels they personally could make a substantial difference locally (19% "major" + 44% "some") or for children in extreme poverty (18% "major" + 34% "some"). Their ambition lags a bit when focusing on global poverty as a whole: The plurality (31%) assumes only a "minor" impact is possible. Non-practicing Christians, however, show patterns of feeling unable to help with these big issues. Just one in four says they personally could affect international poverty on more than a minor level (6% "major," 18% "some").

Though U.S. adults' low awareness of poverty levels might be disconcerting, it shouldn't be assumed that a lack of information goes hand-in-hand with a lack of engagement. Those who say they have volunteered for or donated to end poverty, globally and locally, are not any more likely to have updated, accurate numbers on poverty. The puzzling yet reassuring truth is that many Americans have eagerly partnered with the developing world and contributed to global poverty's decline even while relatively unaware of its nature or extent. Looking forward, the hope and the challenge, specifically for the U.S. Church, are the same: How much broader, richer and more effective could our contributions be if they were also well-informed?

## HOW PEOPLE PRIORITIZE POVERTY

Given the range of causes that present themselves to U.S. adults, how do they prioritize their participation in addressing the world's problems—and poverty among them?

Barna asked respondents to identify social issues they feel are important to personally support. Practicing Christians' responses are generally similar to the national averages, peaking with clean water (89%, compared to 92% average) which has perhaps been mainstreamed by its emphasis in digital campaigns and international development goals in recent years. Practicing Christians also align with all U.S. adults in showing significant attention to child trafficking (88%, compared to 85% average), orphan and foster care (87%, compared to 79% average), education (87% each) and children in extreme poverty (87%, compared to 88% average). Child evangelism (61%) and church-building (67%) are,

## A GLIMPSE OF POVERTY AND PROGRESS

The standard for extreme poverty is living on $1.90 or less per day.

By recent estimates, 10.7% of the world's population, including 2% of the U.S. population, lives in extreme poverty.

Since 1990, the global poverty rate has dropped by 24 percentage points.

One of the United Nations' Millennium Development Goals was to halve the 1990 poverty rate (35%) by 2015. The world accomplished this by 2010.

More than 1 billion people have been lifted out of poverty since 1990.

Additional source: "Poverty Overview," The World Bank. http://www.worldbank.org/en/topic/poverty/overview

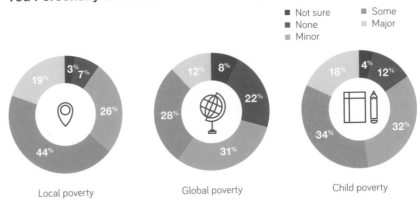

## Practicing Christians: How Much Could You Personally Have an Effect on Poverty?

■ Not sure   ■ Some
■ None   ■ Major
■ Minor

**Local poverty**
3% 7% 26% 44% 19%

**Global poverty**
8% 22% 31% 28% 12%

**Child poverty**
4% 12% 32% 34% 18%

May 2017, *n*=219 U.S. practicing Christians.

understandably, more popular endeavors among this religious group.

Once respondents noted *all* of the issues they believed were important to personally address, they were then asked to hone this list by selecting their *top three* priorities. Though results remain staggered, prompting respondents to be more specific significantly boosted one concern to the top of the list: One in four U.S. adults (25%) prioritizes taking action on childhood education, followed by local poverty (24%) and environmental issues (15%).

There are predictable divergences on social issues that have more political associations, a central theme of responses throughout the survey. Consider how the environment, global warming and refugee response have become major partisan issues, particularly in the time this survey was conducted. Political activism itself is rarely an expressed priority for practicing Christians, so it's not surprising that seemingly politically contentious subjects are among the least popular issues for this group.

Global poverty (6%) stands out among causes that less often inspire personal support. Those of other faiths (15%) are actually more likely than practicing Christians (8%) to feel drawn toward this option, despite Christians' high levels of reported concern for international poverty. It's possible that those of other faiths, which include Islam, Hinduism and Buddhism, are more keenly aware of poor regions in which theirs is the majority religion or still feel a connection to nations from which their families or faith communities emigrated.

One in four U.S. adults prioritizes taking action on childhood education

## General Priorities for Personal Involvement, by Religion

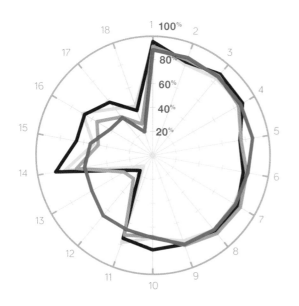

■ Practicing Christians
■ Non-practicing Christians
■ Other faith
░ No faith

1. Clean water
2. Child trafficking
3. Children in extreme poverty
4. Access to education for children
5. Caring for orphans or foster children
6. Local poverty*
7. Medical aid / research
8. Disaster response
9. Special needs (physical or mental)
10. Economic development in poor communities
11. Empowering girls where inequality exists
12. Building churches in other countries
13. Child evangelism
14. Environmental causes
15. International / global poverty*
16. Addressing global warming
17. Refugee response
18. Political activism

May 2017, n=1,001 U.S. adults.

*The broader categories of "international / global poverty" and "local poverty" were presented here neutrally, alongside other issues and causes that could rightfully be categorized as aspects of poverty action.

However, as both global and local poverty were presented neutrally alongside other issues that they technically encompass, specificity in how people would like to help alleviate poverty shouldn't be confused with an apathy toward poverty in general. (See Susan Mettes' column on page 70 for more insight.) In absolute terms, practicing Christians still have poverty on their

## Most Important Cause to Personally Support

*(When asked to select top three)*

- ■ All U.S. adults
- ■ Practicing Christians
- ■ Non-practicing Christians

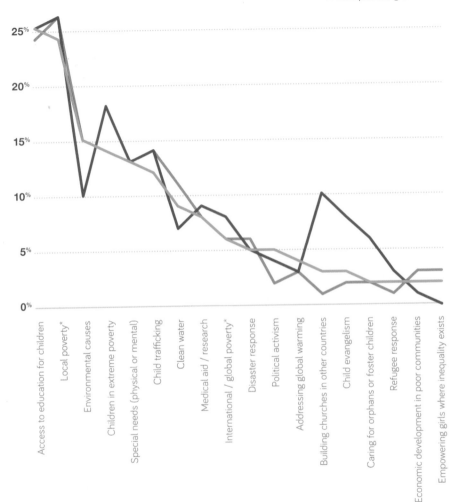

May 2017, *n*=1,001 U.S. adults.

*The broader categories of "international / global poverty" and "local poverty" were presented here neutrally, alongside other issues and causes that could rightfully be categorized as aspects of poverty action.

radar. After all, 26 percent of practicing Christians include local poverty and 18 percent include children in extreme poverty in their top three social issues. Further, even when Christians—and all adults, for that matter—do not select the general categories about poverty, they indicate a desire for personal involvement in a number of interventions that prevent poverty or its noneconomic symptoms. Direct, specific actions appear more manageable than aiming to address "global poverty" as a broad category, which can feel like an amorphous, overwhelming task to prioritize. For example, practicing Christians are even more motivated to personally undertake initiatives related to helping children. They fall in line with all U.S. adults in emphasizing education (25%), then round out their top three social issues with children in extreme poverty (18%) and child trafficking (14%).

## Americans Weigh the Solutions

There is no one-size-fits-all fix for poverty, and an overwhelming number of anti-poverty agencies address the issue from various angles. Many of these organizations agree with UNICEF that the best way to address poverty is early in life, with young children—a promising approach, given the attention the public says they give to such causes, as already mentioned in this report.[10] But efforts to reduce poverty take myriad forms.

When asked what might be most effective in alleviating poverty, U.S. adults point to the same issue in which they would prefer to be involved: education. One in four (25%) sees this as the best route. They believe least in the power of spiritual health to address poverty (38% "least effective").

**PUT IT TO USE**

**Think**

This study indicates that specific rather than vague goals could seem more approachable or manageable to donors and volunteers. For pastors looking to energize the compassion and generosity of congregants, it helps to be precise.

**Ask**

Does your church rally around any specific long-term giving projects? Are there organizations that your congregants already represent or support that you could highlight or partner with?

**Do**

Church leaders, choose one or two issues to focus on for at least the next year. Plan specific moments to highlight the cause and communicate clear, measurable goals. Maybe an expert could be a guest speaker and help present a particular project within the framework of poverty alleviation.

## How Much Will Each Help People Out of Poverty?

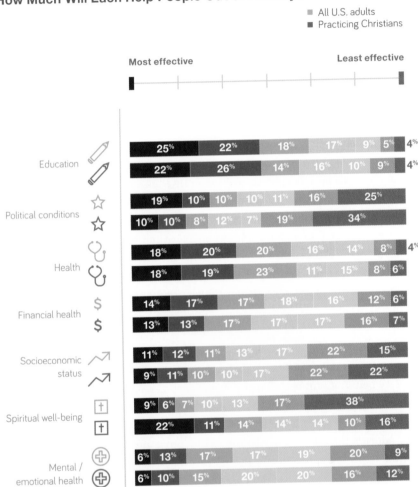

All U.S. adults
Practicing Christians

Most effective — Least effective

**Education**
All U.S. adults: 25% | 22% | 18% | 17% | 9% | 5% | 4%
Practicing Christians: 22% | 26% | 14% | 16% | 10% | 9% | 4%

**Political conditions**
All U.S. adults: 19% | 10% | 10% | 10% | 11% | 16% | 25%
Practicing Christians: 10% | 10% | 8% | 12% | 7% | 19% | 34%

**Health**
All U.S. adults: 18% | 20% | 20% | 16% | 14% | 8% | 4%
Practicing Christians: 18% | 19% | 23% | 11% | 15% | 8% | 6%

**Financial health**
All U.S. adults: 14% | 17% | 17% | 18% | 16% | 12% | 6%
Practicing Christians: 13% | 13% | 17% | 17% | 17% | 16% | 7%

**Socioeconomic status**
All U.S. adults: 11% | 12% | 11% | 13% | 17% | 22% | 15%
Practicing Christians: 9% | 11% | 10% | 10% | 17% | 22% | 22%

**Spiritual well-being**
All U.S. adults: 9% | 6% | 7% | 10% | 13% | 17% | 38%
Practicing Christians: 22% | 11% | 14% | 14% | 14% | 10% | 16%

**Mental / emotional health**
All U.S. adults: 6% | 13% | 17% | 17% | 19% | 20% | 9%
Practicing Christians: 6% | 10% | 15% | 20% | 20% | 16% | 12%

May 2017, *n*=1,001 U.S. adults.

Practicing Christians view things differently; they give quite a lot of credit to spiritual health for lifting people out of poverty. More than one in five (22%) calls this the most effective solution, tying with education. On many other issues, including mental well-being, finances and socioeconomic status, their views are similar to all U.S. adults, though they put very little stock in political conditions (34% "least effective").

The general population is split on the influence of politics in poverty; though one-quarter (25%) calls it the least impactful answer, one-fifth gives an opposite assessment (19% say it's "most effective").

There are good reasons to pursue each one of these methods at some point while attempting to improve a person's life and work against poverty. Many humanitarian organizations advocate for a holistic approach that incorporates multiple interventions: education, medicine, financial instruction, mental and emotional health, political conditions, socioeconomic status and spiritual well-being.

## ASSIGNING RESPONSIBILITY FOR POVERTY

The groups and programs that can be acknowledged for limiting poverty's reach are many and belong to various institutions. In the U.S., government programs such as Medicare and Social Security have been credited by some for lifting many out of poverty.[11] Meanwhile, the efforts of non-governmental organizations such as the Rockefeller Foundation have been credited with the Green Revolution, which raised crop yields in Asia and Mexico dramatically.[12] Businesses have implemented interventions such as iodized salt, which raised the average IQ in the United States,[13] and Fortune 500 companies see mutual advantage in pushing against corruption and for jobs in poor countries.[14]

Sometimes the illness and the cure are provided by the same body. For instance, any student of humanitarian efforts will have heard that famine is a political problem,[15] especially in an age when there is enough food for everyone on earth.[16] While poverty and corruption do go hand-in-hand,[17] poor governments often spend much of their income as major employers and have difficulty balancing the overhead expense with services to citizens.[18] The story of global poverty, in other words, is complicated.

One aspect of poverty reduction, on the surface, does appear simple to U.S. adults, including Christians: They count on the government to take the lead in addressing it. All U.S. adults and practicing Christians are most likely to say the government of the country needing aid bears primary responsibility (39% and 33%, respectively). Almost equal numbers of each group say it falls on the shoulders of non-profit and humanitarian organizations, whether international (29% U.S. adults, 31% practicing Christians) or local (8% U.S. adults, 6% practicing Christians).

Opinions about the parties that are ultimately responsible correlate to a

More than one in five practicing Christians calls spiritual health the most effective poverty solution

U.S. adults, including Christians, count on the government to take the lead in addressing poverty

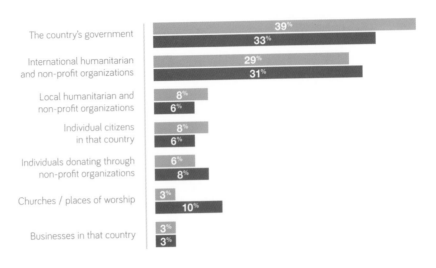

## Who Is Primarily Responsible for Reducing Global Poverty?

■ All U.S. adults
■ Practicing Christians

The country's government
39%
33%

International humanitarian and non-profit organizations
29%
31%

Local humanitarian and non-profit organizations
8%
6%

Individual citizens in that country
8%
6%

Individuals donating through non-profit organizations
6%
8%

Churches / places of worship
3%
10%

Businesses in that country
3%
3%

May 2017, *n*=1,001 U.S. adults.

sense of personal influence as well. Those who defer to governments as responsible for global poverty are less likely than others to believe they can personally have an impact on global poverty, with only one in five (20%) saying they can make more than a minor difference. Those who think non-profits carry primary responsibility have only moderately better opinions of their own potential impact (7% "major" + 27% "some" difference). Meanwhile, those who think churches or individuals are primarily responsible are much more convinced that they too can make a difference (47% and 45%, respectively).

If anyone holds churches accountable for addressing global poverty, it's Christians, and evangelicals most of all (17%). On the other hand, only one percent of people with no faith and none of those who subscribe to other religions believe that churches are primarily responsible for dealing with poverty overseas. Any sense that addressing extreme poverty is a responsibility of the Church comes from within the Church. Christians promote this strategy even more so for *domestic* poverty; one-third of evangelicals (32%) feels churches hold primary responsibility. Practicing Christians (15%) affirm this to a smaller degree, though still three times more than all U.S. adults (5%), and

Any sense that addressing poverty is a responsibility of the Church comes from within the Church

at a significant jump from the 6 percent of practicing Christians who felt this way in 2007.

These responses correspond to a Christian understanding that the Church has an obligation to the poor and that faith is integral in poverty alleviation. Self-identified Christians are generally in agreement that the Bible directly instructs them to help those living in poverty (79% agree at least somewhat), and practicing Christians assert this truth with even more force (47% strongly agree). Most also have a conviction that anti-poverty work is beneficial for both the recipients and those ministering to or providing for them. A majority of Christians (84%) agrees to some extent that "helping the poor helps Christians understand the heart of Christ more deeply." Again, practicing Christians are even more likely to cling to these spiritual constructs of anti-poverty efforts (57% agree strongly, 37% agree somewhat).

Some Christians see anti-poverty work as the litmus test for sincere faith: They believe that on one side, there are Christians who are actively working to help the poor, and on the other side ... well, there are people who "are not true Christians." This firm stance isn't widely accepted. Similar

## Practicing Christians Rate Spiritual Poverty Concepts

■ Strongly agree    ■ Somewhat disagree
■ Somewhat agree    ■ Strongly disagree

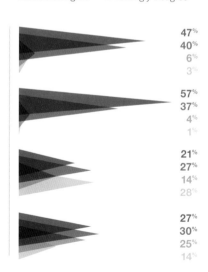

"The Bible teaches that Christians should help children living in poverty"

47%
40%
6%
3%

"Helping the poor helps Christians understand the heart of Christ more deeply"

57%
37%
4%
1%

"Poverty is an inevitable result of the sin of man and will exist until Christ returns"

21%
27%
14%
28%

"If Christians are not helping the poor and vulnerable, they aren't true Christians"

27%
30%
25%
14%

May 2017, n=219 practicing Christians.

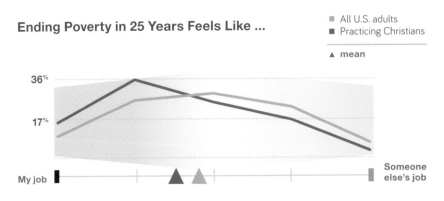

**Ending Poverty in 25 Years Feels Like ...**

■ All U.S. adults
■ Practicing Christians

▲ mean

36%

17%

My job                Someone else's job

May 2017, *n*=1,001 U.S. adults, 219 practicing Christians.

percentages fall across the spectrum of agreement (22% strongly agree, 27% somewhat agree, 25% somewhat disagree, 23% strongly disagree). In this case, practicing Christians are a little more willing to set this standard; 57 percent agree at least somewhat that authentic Christians are those who help the impoverished.

An idea that gains less traction among believers is that poverty is somehow inevitable, the result of the sin of man and a blight on creation until Christ's return. More than a third of Christians (37%) disagrees strongly with this perspective. Practicing Christians are slightly more resigned to this idea; one-fifth (21%) strongly agrees.

Ultimately, viewing poverty as predestined and permanent doesn't jibe with Christians' confidence that it can be overcome—and that they can help. At another point in the survey, Barna asked respondents to indicate on a sliding scale whether the task of ending global poverty—specifically within the next 25 years—falls on them or someone else. Overall, Americans' views on this duty have been clarified over the last few years, moving more to the precise ends of the scale—"my job" or "someone else's job"—rather than a shared middle. More than U.S. adults in general, practicing Christians feel a sense of personal responsibility to help end poverty (53%, 17% of whom do so entirely).

## THE BIG QUESTION: CAN WE END POVERTY?

Before moving on to look at the ways that people actually use their time and resources to confront poverty, Barna wanted to know: Do people *really* believe that the problem of poverty could cease to exist—within our lifetime?

When given a sliding scale to describe how they feel about ending poverty in the next 25 years, equal percentages of U.S. adults (15%) select either extreme—definitely "doable" or "not doable"—though a majority leans toward this outcome being feasible. Though Americans tend to see this mission as "inspiring" (29% at the highest level) they are still completely split on whether it is "believable" or "not believable" (45% fall on either side of the scale, 10% are neutral).

Practicing Christians' optimism about defeating poverty is rising with time; on all points, there is a roughly 10-percentage-point increase in the view that ending poverty in the next quarter of a century is an extremely worthy and realistic goal.

Younger generations are more inclined to think positively about poverty's potential end. Millennials surpass other generations in feeling the highest degree of inspiration and are most likely to find the idea of ending poverty extremely doable. Meanwhile, Elders are twice as likely as Millennials to think it's not possible to end poverty in 25 years, and few Elders are very inspired by this goal.

Some of the most privileged groups of Americans are unfortunately the least likely to have high hopes about the global poverty fight. For instance, ethnic minorities are more likely than white Americans to rate the idea of ending poverty as highly inspirational (35% vs. 26%), believable (23% vs. 13%) and doable (21% vs. 12%).

Educated adults usually have muted responses to these questions. College graduates are less likely to regard the idea of ending poverty as very inspirational (24%, compared to 33% of high school graduates). The proportion of U.S. adults who see ending poverty as extremely believable declines significantly for those who have completed even some college (16%, compared to 25% of high school graduates) and continues to drop among those who are college graduates (11%). Prosperous groups are also less likely to have a positive outlook on poverty, even though it could be argued they have greater resources to tackle the problem. Those who make less than $50,000 a year—which, on the lower end of the scale, would include some considered to be living in poverty themselves—are more likely than higher earners to find the idea of ending poverty extremely inspirational (33% vs. 26% who earn $50,000–$100,000), believable (21% vs. 14) and doable (19% vs. 13%).

Younger generations and minorities are more confident that poverty can be overcome

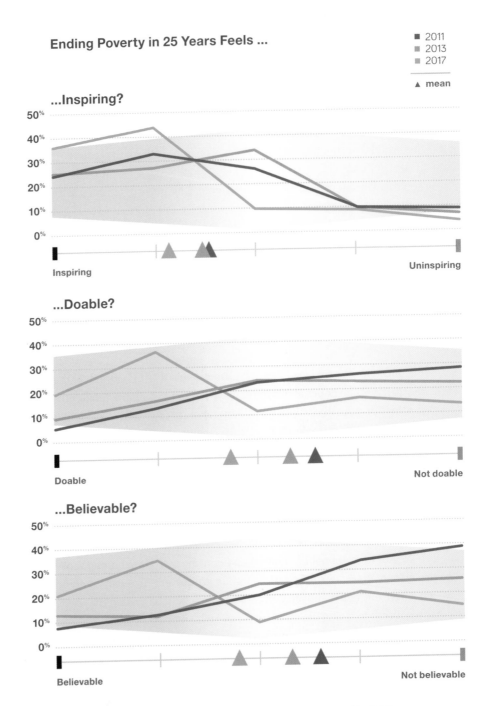

Ending Poverty in 25 Years Feels ...

■ 2011
■ 2013
■ 2017

▲ mean

...Inspiring?

Inspiring                                     Uninspiring

...Doable?

Doable                                        Not doable

...Believable?

Believable                                    Not believable

2011, *n*=270 practicing Christians; 2013, *n*=249 practicing Christians; May 2017, *n*=219 practicing Christians.

## Generational Hopes for Ending Poverty

*(% who chose the highest level of optimism on a sliding scale)*

■ Millennials   ■ Boomers
■ Gen X   ■ Elders

"To me, ending global poverty in the next 25 years feels …"

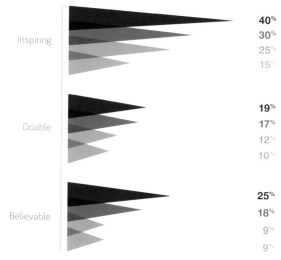

| | |
|---|---|
| Inspiring | 40% |
| | 30% |
| | 25% |
| | 15% |
| Doable | 19% |
| | 17% |
| | 12% |
| | 10% |
| Believable | 25% |
| | 18% |
| | 9% |
| | 9% |

May 2017. *n*=1,001 U.S. adults.

In the following chapter, we'll cover how those with firsthand experiences of poverty are the most trusted voices on the subject. This is another piece of good news, as those who are marginalized or touched by poverty cling to their confidence that it can be overcome—and hope remains a valuable currency in addressing global scarcity.

## PUT IT TO USE

### Think

U.S. adults with more education are typically less concerned or optimistic about ending poverty. It's possible that being exposed to *many* ideas leaves one struggling to see urgency or hope in *particular* issues, especially in light of how overwhelming the world's problems are.

### Do

Highly educated adults—who less often live in poverty themselves, yet may have more resources to give to those in need—could use reminders of the tangible, positive impact of their contributions. Encouraging volunteering and elevating impoverished voices fosters relational (not just intellectual or financial) engagement in anti-poverty work.

## AN IDEOLOGICAL IMPASSE

When politics and faith mix, it has a confounding—and sometimes counterintuitive—influence on how people address poverty

As in most discussions about complex topics in the U.S. today, political ideologies prove divisive when it comes to poverty. Simply put: Conservatives and liberals hold very different beliefs on the subject of poverty. They disagree on the root causes of poverty. They disagree on who should be responsible for caring for the poor. They disagree on which issues of poverty are most urgent. They disagree, even, on the reasons people *don't* donate to the poor. These beliefs, inevitably, affect people's actual engagement around fighting poverty as well.

The issue of poverty is certainly not a politically neutral one, and those politics seep into churches. While serving the poor may not seem like a controversial issue for Christians—scripture is, after all, very clear on the Church's mandate to do so—the *what, how, why* and *who* are greatly influenced by a Christian's political leaning. Thus, pastors, unfortunately, must be aware of the political minefields surrounding issues of poverty and learn to navigate them effectively. In doing so, hopefully churches can be united through their work for the poor—not divided by it.

Let's take a look at how politics influences issues around poverty—both within and without the Church.

## *What* Is Our Responsibility?

Practicing Christians—regardless of whether they are liberal or conservative—are more likely to take responsibility for serving the poor. This is good news for pastors and churches! However, conservatives and liberals overall (both inside and outside the Church) differ on what they believe is their personal responsibility. They also have a deep ideological difference in what they see as the barriers to taking personal action against poverty.

In general, liberals express more concern than conservatives around issues of poverty. Americans who identify as politically liberal are twice as likely to report extreme concern for global poverty (37% vs. 19% of self-identified political conservatives). Conservatives—especially Boomers and Elders—are much less inclined to say it's important to be personally involved on global poverty (43% vs. 71%). Conservatives tend to be more concerned with local

Practicing Christians—regardless of political ideology—are more likely to take responsibility for serving the poor

## Liberal vs. Conservative Interest in Global Poverty

■ All conservatives
■ All liberals

43%
71%

Consider it important to personally volunteer or donate for international poverty

19%
37%

Extremely concerned about global poverty

May 2017, *n*=1,001 U.S. adults.

poverty—though still at slightly lower levels than liberals (78% vs. 83%).

Things change when you look only at practicing Christians. Active faith has a strong positive influence on people's engagement with the poor, regardless of political ideology. It's important to note that Christian conservatives far outnumber practicing Christian liberals—about half of practicing Christians consider themselves conservative, one-third is moderate, and only one in seven says their beliefs about political and social issues are liberal. Due to the small sample size of practicing Christians with liberal social values, Barna has combined them with moderates here for the purpose of analysis. The results show that an active faith indeed produces some consistency in ideas about and engagement with the poor.

Some gaps do remain between conservative and moderate / liberal practicing Christians in their reported activities, and even more so in their mindsets. Though the presence of an active faith increases the chance that non-conservatives will feel concern about poverty or other issues, it has less effect among conservatives. For instance, nearly half of practicing Christians who identify as liberal or moderate (42%) express extreme concern about global poverty, while conservative practicing Christians align with the average American (26%).

Beyond their expressed levels of concern, practicing Christians, regardless of political ideology, are more likely than all other respondents of their same political leanings to report getting involved. Among liberals, that usually means

## Interest in Global Poverty, by Ideology & Faith Engagement

■ Practicing Christian conservatives  ■ Practicing Christian liberals and moderates
■ Conservatives, not practicing Christian  ■ Liberals and moderates, not practicing Christian

49%
40%
61%
56%

Consider it important to
personally volunteer or donate for
international poverty

26%
16%
42%
24%

Extremely concerned about
global poverty

May 2017, *n*=1,001 U.S. adults (including 109 practicing Christian moderates and liberals combined, 110 practicing Christian conservatives, 218 conservatives who are not practicing Christians and 564 liberals and moderates who are not practicing Christians).

When asked what keeps people from taking actions to reduce poverty, liberals highlight a lack of hope and conservatives highlight a lack of trust

volunteering more time; among conservatives, that usually means donating more dollars. This spike in engagement is directed toward a variety of causes, particularly places of worship.

So what is it that *stops* people from engaging? Relevant for pastors and spiritual leaders who are working to activate their congregants around issues of poverty, conservatives and liberals point to fundamentally different roots for their skepticism. When asked what keeps people from taking actions to reduce poverty, liberals highlight a lack of hope and conservatives highlight a lack of trust. While liberals indicate people might hold back because they don't know where to

start (40%), don't believe poverty is solvable (40%) or doubt their own ability to make a difference (39%), conservatives assume the greatest obstacles are a lack of confidence in the governments of poor countries (36%), in non-profit organizations (33%) or in the wisdom of spending on foreign rather than domestic concerns (33%).

## *How* Do We Best Fight Poverty?

One thing both liberals and conservatives agree on: It's not an individual's job to fight global poverty—and, in fact, the two groups share a sense of personal helplessness. Fewer than one in 10 from either ideological camp agrees to the statement,

## Active Faith Connects to Action, Regardless of Ideology

■ Practicing Christian conservatives    ■ Practicing Christian liberals and moderates
■ Conservatives, not practicing Christian    ■ Liberals and moderates, not practicing Christian

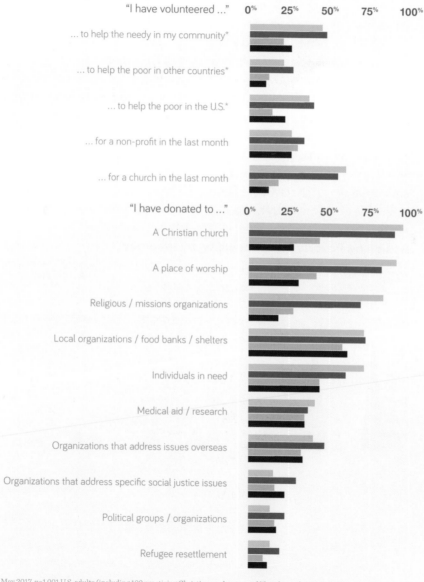

May 2017, n=1,001 U.S. adults (including 109 practicing Christian moderates and liberals combined, 110 practicing Christian conservatives, 218 conservatives who are not practicing Christians and 564 liberals and moderates who are not practicing Christians).

"I could have a major influence on global poverty." Accordingly, just 6 percent of each group assign primary responsibility for global poverty to individuals donating through non-profit organizations.

However, when you expand beyond personal responsibility to liberals' and conservatives' ideas of who (or what) is accountable for global poverty, some important distinctions emerge. While both liberals (37%) and conservatives (33%) feel the governments in poor nations are crucial in caring for their poor, liberals lean on non-profits (39%

vs. 24% of conservatives), whereas conservatives are more likely than liberals to consider churches (7% vs. 2% of liberals) or individual citizens of that nation (12% vs. 6% of liberals) as an authority. Unsurprisingly, practicing Christians in each group are slightly more likely to place responsibility on churches (14% of practicing Christian conservatives and 6% of practicing Christian moderates and liberals).

## Why Does Poverty Exist?

Perhaps the greatest ideological divide between conservatives and

### Assigning Poverty Responsibility, by Ideology

*Who is primarily responsible for addressing global poverty?*

■ All conservatives
■ All liberals

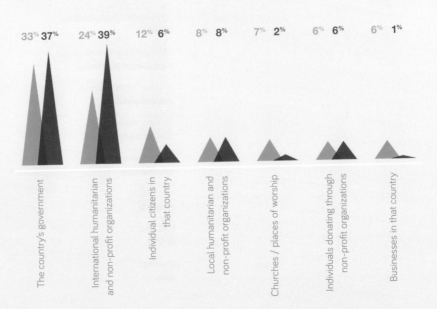

33% 37%    24% 39%    12% 6%    8% 8%    7% 2%    6% 6%    6% 1%

The country's government | International humanitarian and non-profit organizations | Individual citizens in that country | Local humanitarian and non-profit organizations | Churches / places of worship | Individuals donating through non-profit organizations | Businesses in that country

May 2017, *n*=606 U.S. adults.

liberals on the subject of poverty is *why* it exists in the first place. Conservatives believe individuals have a significant measure of agency in their situation, whereas liberals point to broader, systemic issues as the cause for poverty. More than half of conservatives (52%) feel "everyone has an equal opportunity to climb out of poverty, and no one has to be poor," an idea that less than a third of liberals (31%) supports. One in four conservatives (26%), versus 17 percent of liberals, attributes poverty to a person's laziness or unwillingness to work. The proportion of conservatives who disagree that poverty could be caused by a lack of sensitivity to human need (54%) or the greed of powerful, wealthy nations (51%) doubles that of liberals (27% and 22%, respectively). Conservatives are also more inclined toward the idea that "poverty is an inevitable result of the sin of man and will exist until Christ returns" (42% agree, compared to 32% of liberals).

## Who Should We Help?

There are poignant divides between liberals and conservatives when it comes to who and what they choose to support in the fight against poverty. It's not hard to see the connections to political messaging reflected in conservatives' comparatively low general interest in supporting environmental causes (56%, compared to 85% of liberals) economic development in poor countries (63%, compared to 81% of liberals), empowering girls (62%, compared to 84% of liberals), refugee response (31%, compared to 67% of liberals) and global warming (37%, compared to 85% of liberals). On less politically entrenched topics, conservatives are more inclined to be supportive, though still at consistently lower rates than liberals. This trend continues with activities specific to anti-poverty efforts overseas, including education, social empowerment for children, economic development, job skills or general assistance to the poor.

A general link between religious groups and conservative values becomes apparent elsewhere, as conservatives are more likely than liberals to personally prioritize the causes of child evangelism (44% vs. 32%) and church-building (45% vs. 29%). This also surfaces in their reported donations: Conservatives say they give to missions organizations (47% vs. 25%) and churches (60% vs. 31%) more often than liberals.

## An Opportunity for Unity

This particular survey can't fully parse the many ways in which religion and politics intermingle in

## Choosing the Important Issues to Personally Support, by Ideology

■ All conservatives
■ All liberals

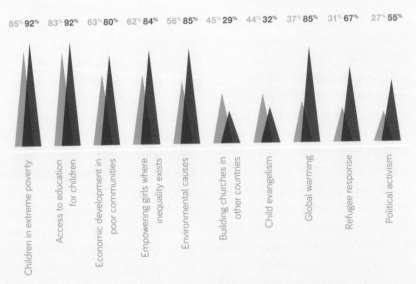

| 85% **92%** | 83% **92%** | 63% **80%** | 62% **84%** | 56% **85%** | 45% **29%** | 44% **32%** | 37% **85%** | 31% **67%** | 27% **55%** |

Children in extreme poverty / Access to education for children / Economic development in poor communities / Empowering girls where inequality exists / Environmental causes / Building churches in other countries / Child evangelism / Global warming / Refugee response / Political activism

May 2017, *n*=606 U.S. adults.

the U.S. But it does show that being a practicing Christian at least increases the likelihood of feeling that the Church bears responsibility for global poverty (14% of conservative practicing Christians, 6% of moderate and liberal practicing Christians), looking for biblical perspectives on how the American Church should be involved in social justice (53% of conservative practicing Christians, 38% of moderate and liberal practicing Christians) and seeing pastors as credible sources on the topic (53% of conservative practicing Christians, 56%

of moderate and liberal practicing Christians say "definitely"). In particular, moderates and liberals—those outside the Church and especially those within the Church—are looking for the Church to do *more* in the fight against global poverty.

From this data emerges a challenge and an opportunity for today's pastors, particularly those in evangelical and conservative circles: to not abdicate this authority solely to non-governmental and non-profit organizations. Rather, faith leaders might ask themselves: *In my sermons, campaigns, charity*

## Spiritual and Political Attitudes Toward Poverty

■ Practicing Christian conservatives
■ Conservatives, not practicing Christian
■ Practicing Christian liberals and moderates
■ Liberals and moderates, not practicing Christian

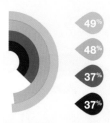

49%
48%
37%
37%

"My church / place of worship should be more involved in helping the global poor"**

% who "strongly" agree
**asked of those who ever attend a church or other place of worship
May 2017, n=1,001 U.S. adults (including 109 practicing Christian moderates and liberals combined, 110 practicing Christian conservatives, 218 conservatives who are not practicing Christians and 564 liberals and moderates who are not practicing Christians)

*partnerships and personal life, how can I be an attentive and creative advocate of poverty reduction?* Many conservative parishioners are ready to lend their ear and trust their dollars to their church on this issue—in fact, they likely see it as the best "funnel" for their donations and compassion.

Additionally, when ministers take the lead in helping the poor, it could provide a rare connection point for liberals who otherwise feel conflicted about or dismissive of

the role of the Church. Disaffected or isolated Christian liberals and moderates—perhaps even some in the "spiritual but not religious" category—may welcome a reminder that there is a place not only for them, but also for their passion for social justice in the local church.

When political demarcations mar communities, families, workplaces, media—and, yes, churches—faith leaders have a profound duty to communicate the truth about poverty. Conservatives and liberals, even Christian ones, may fundamentally disagree on many policies and opinions. But caring for the poor is central to Jesus' teaching, and pastors who take this to heart help bridge two devastating divides in U.S. culture: one between the majority of Christian conservatives and a call for embodied care of the poor, and another between the majority of liberals and active membership in a community that encourages their generosity. When church leaders reach out to the poor, they offer a message that reaches across American ideologies and affiliations as well.

When church leaders reach out to the poor, they offer a message that reaches across American ideologies and affiliations as well

# A UNITED EFFORT IN POVERTY REDUCTION

## Q&A WITH MICHELE WYMER

Michele advises non-profit and corporate clients regarding international policy affairs and global development projects. As a partner with the DC-based Kyle House Group, Michele provides strategic guidance for clients seeking government relations counsel, commercial advocacy, partnership development and policy analysis that improves the lives of people around the world. Previously, Michele served as a senior staff member on the State and Foreign Operations Subcommittee of the U.S. Senate Appropriations Committee, traveling extensively to conduct oversight of U.S. foreign assistance programs in more than 60 countries. In this capacity, Michele was charged with authoring the annual legislation that determined operational and programming funding levels for U.S. foreign assistance programs.

**MICHELE WYMER**
Partner with
Kyle House Group

Q What do you want the general public to better understand about the ways in which governments and non-governmental organizations (NGOs) can work together? Are there any common misconceptions you encounter about the responsibilities of either when it comes to addressing poverty?

The percentage the U.S. government spends on U.S. foreign assistance and what those dollars pay for is one of the biggest misconceptions. When polled, most Americans believe our government spends upwards of 25 percent of the federal budget on foreign assistance. This could not be further from the truth. Just 1 percent of federal dollars go to foreign assistance, and the portion dedicated to alleviating poverty, disease and hunger and meeting humanitarian aid is only half of that. Of that 1 percent of the budget, around 70 percent of that is spent in partnerships with NGOs that implement programs to address global poverty, increase diplomacy and development capacities. This is to benefit the host country, who also have an interest in a healthier and more economically secure population.[19]

NGOs are the best partners in every country around the globe at effectively administering resources to address the most critical and pressing needs. They are the partners that are the issue experts and relied upon heavily by our government and others to effectively deliver services.

Q When Americans are asked to identify the causes they'd like to personally support, issues regarding vulnerable children routinely top the list. U.S. adults also widely consider education to be the most effective way to alleviate poverty. As an expert in the field, are they correct in their instincts that early intervention is important?

Yes, all evidence points to early intervention as one of the critical life-saving and giving interventions. Thought leaders like the Bill and Melinda Gates Foundation, UNICEF and others have created entire strategies and funding mechanisms that support this theory. Evidence shows that the first 1,000 days of a person's life are critical to setting up healthy minds and bodies. Early interventions like nutrition and access to water in sanitation in the first 1,000 days (conception to 2nd birthday) set children up to succeed. The 1,000 Days Campaign states: "Globally, almost half of all child deaths are due to malnutrition and it is now estimated that one-third of the world's population is malnourished—suffering from either undernutrition, obesity, deficiencies in essential vitamins and minerals or some combination of all three."[20]

The hardest statistic to swallow is that malnutrition and its effects are entirely preventable, but the damage done is irreversible. Programs that address the first 1,000 days and educate moms on how they can best provide for themselves and their babies during that critical window are having massive impacts. According to UNICEF, the under-five mortality rate has been cut in half since 1990.[21] Despite these impressive results, the fact remains that 15,000 children under five die every day of preventable diseases, and according to the Food and Agricultural Organization of the United Nations, 155 million children under the age of five are affected by stunting.[22] So while there is hope in how far we've come, there is certainly more to be done. Early interventions like good sanitation measures and breastfeeding also have proven track records in providing benefits for both mom and baby.

Q The data highlights some striking differences in the ways conservatives and liberals see and engage with poverty. How has your work in DC either confirmed or contradicted these attitudes within the general public? Though liberals and conservatives, by definition, will disagree on some methods and policies, where do you see the common ground on this issue?

Yes, there are certainly varying degrees of separation between how liberals and conservatives view poverty. Generally, liberals believe that the government should be responsible for *all* services, including providing all types of services to the poor. Republicans believe that, while many services need to be in place, the government should be smaller, taking a more hands-off approach. That is where the divide lives: Who should pay—U.S. taxes? Or should we rely on the goodness of others while also expecting people to pull themselves up out of addiction, homelessness, joblessness, etc.?

That is why faith-based and local charities are incredibly important to both sides of the aisle, and generally very well-respected. According to Faith for International Assistance, for every $1 invested from the U.S. government, American faith-based organizations (FBOs) raise nearly $6.[23] FBOs typically provide services to the most marginalized populations—homeless, hungry, sick, elderly—domestic and abroad, and NGOs and FBOs are the on-the-ground implementers.

Those motivated by faith are inspired by something outside themselves, and that is a uniting force, and an area where the moral argument resonates along with economic, security and other reasons. The challenge is helping the faith community understand how critical their voice and contributions are to protecting marginalized populations, and educating everyday Americans on the critical relationship of private and public resources that, when leveraged, can make the most significant impact for good globally.

"Faith-based and local charities are incredibly important to both sides of the aisle, and generally very well-respected."

# WHY EARLY INTERVENTION MATTERS

## Q&A WITH DR. DAN BREWSTER

Dan advises the Nazarene Compassionate Ministries in their child development programs. For 30 years, Dan worked with Compassion International and recently retired from the role of director for their international Holistic Child Development (HCD) ministries. He is credited with coining the term "4–14 Window," to refer to the importance of reaching children during the spiritually formative time between ages 4 and 14. He has traveled to over 100 countries and been involved in planning and monitoring child and family development for relief projects in more than 50 countries. Dan and his wife, Alice, have lived in Penang, Malaysia for the past 19 years. He has a doctorate in missiology from Fuller Seminary and has written and taught widely, promoting and managing Christian HCD ministries and programs.

**DR. DAN BREWSTER**
Advisor for Nazarene
Compassionate Ministries

Q  What could you share from your own research and experience as to why a concern for and focus on children is a powerful approach in poverty reduction?

Community development often has an adult bias. This bias may be a mistake in terms of effectiveness even for development purposes. For many years, UNICEF research has consistently indicated that *the* most significant interventions for national development are child health and education.[24] My work in Compassion bore this out. Though we did not call our work "community development" and our funds did not assist in broad community development activities, our child development projects, if well-designed and managed, often resulted in better quality community development outcomes. We found that communities could often unite around the needs of their children even though other issues were divisive. Parents joined together to make improvements to schools, water supplies and roads as a response to the challenges of their children. The community provided the context for our ministries and many of the essential resources. So even if our objective is to relieve poverty on a national or community scale, we do well to focus primarily on ministry to children.

"Communities could often unite around the needs of their children even though other issues were divisive."

Q What are unique issues facing children around the world living in extreme poverty?

Poverty goes beyond finances, so addressing it must go beyond material assistance as well. I believe that children and families are best helped when they are becoming the whole person that God intends them to be. That means providing nutritious food, education, health care and an understanding of biblical truths. That requires a monetary investment at some point, of course. Many people, including my wife and myself, give to sponsor children and to address the many problems they face. These financial investments are important—but they aren't the sole solution. Ultimately, the goal for every human, whether they live in poverty or prosperity, is that they would come to know that they are made in the image of God and they can use the resources that God has provided to make a difference, in their own lives and the lives of others.

# THE PARTS WE PLAY

2

## HOW INDIVIDUALS AND CHURCHES IN THE U.S. ARE CONFRONTING POVERTY

Many people are willing to pitch in their time and resources, whether or not they feel poverty work falls solely to them. For instance, while just one in eight U.S. adults (12%) tells Barna that they believe individuals bear *primary* responsibility to address domestic poverty, about twice as many (24%) take action through volunteering, and 62 percent say they give money to local organizations like shelters or food banks. They're ready to tackle the problem without necessarily regarding themselves as the solution. Perhaps the saying really does epitomize Americans' sentiment: *Doing something is always better than doing nothing.*

This chapter looks at the many ways that Americans—specifically those who are active in church—are forging ahead in the fight against poverty.

## GIVING MONEY FOR POVERTY

In a 2016 Barna study in partnership with Thrivent Financial, one in nine U.S. Christians who attend church at least annually (11%) said that their ultimate financial goal is to have enough money to give charitably, and a similar percentage (10%) hopes to serve God with their money. Nearly three-quarters of U.S. adults overall (72%) said that generosity is very or extremely important to them.[25]

Comparing to this study, some of Americans' altruistic intentions extend to addressing poverty specifically. On average, the typical American reports donating $434 in the past year to causes or organizations that help children in extreme poverty, with a range of $0 up to $65,000. When non-donors are excluded, the average annual donation rises to $809. Still, nearly half of U.S. adults (46%) do not report donating any money for child poverty in the last year.[26]

The most commonly reported donations are $50 and $100 (each with 7% of all U.S. adults, 13% of donors) or $20 (5% of U.S. adults, 9% of donors) per year.

## Amounts Donated for Child Poverty, by Percentage of U.S. Adults

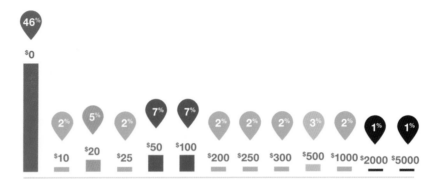

May 2017, n=1,001 U.S. adults.

## Giving Habits of Christians

Personal involvement in confronting poverty goes hand-in-hand with Christianity—*practicing* Christianity, that is. When it comes to anti-poverty work, active Christianity, rather than notional Christianity, makes all the difference. While Christians are sometimes equally involved as those of other faiths, self-identified Christians who do not participate in church life and / or do not say their faith is very important to them show patterns of involvement much more similar to non-religious U.S. adults.

For practicing Christians, it starts in the heart: One in three (34%) says that they are very concerned about global poverty, significantly more than the one in five non-practicing Christians (20%) who share this interest. The burden that practicing Christians feel regarding poverty naturally manifests in their lifestyles. Indeed, the reported donations of practicing Christians far exceed the average of all U.S. adults and other faith segments, with a mean of $839 given to children in extreme poverty each year.

A majority of those in the pews on any given Sunday (91%) says they've given money to church, likely because the tithe and offering are acknowledged or collected regularly, if not weekly. While that doesn't necessarily equate to a poverty gift, such giving may sometimes be applied to charity and anti-poverty efforts, especially considering that many practicing Christians believe the church has a primary role in addressing global poverty. Further,

*Personal involvement in confronting poverty goes hand-in-hand with practicing Christianity*

sizeable majorities of practicing Christians give to missions (75%), local organizations that take care of people in need (70%) and directly to individuals who require assistance (64%). In all categories, practicing Christians outgive their non-practicing peers, and they are 14 percentage points more likely to donate to organizations that address issues overseas.

Evangelicals are also more likely than other faith groups to have donated to a church (93%), missions organizations (81%) and those in need (72%), showing consistency as a group in whether they give and what they give toward.

## To Which Organizations Do Christians Donate?

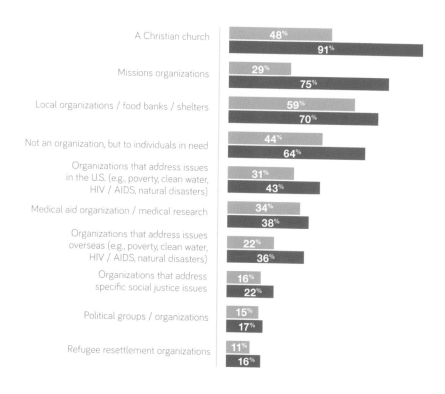

■ Non-practicing Christians
■ Practicing Christians

A Christian church
48%
91%

Missions organizations
29%
75%

Local organizations / food banks / shelters
59%
70%

Not an organization, but to individuals in need
44%
64%

Organizations that address issues in the U.S. (e.g., poverty, clean water, HIV / AIDS, natural disasters)
31%
43%

Medical aid organization / medical research
34%
38%

Organizations that address issues overseas (e.g., poverty, clean water, HIV / AIDS, natural disasters)
22%
36%

Organizations that address specific social justice issues
16%
22%

Political groups / organizations
15%
17%

Refugee resettlement organizations
11%
16%

May 2017, n=219 practicing Christians, 429 non-practicing Christians.

Refugee resettlement is the cause Christians are least likely to financially invest in. This is interesting considering that, since 2016, Barna's data indicates a remarkable softening in Americans' ideas toward refugees, across most faith groups as well: Among practicing Christians alone, the percentage of those who agree the U.S. should welcome refugees more than doubled in one year (from 16% to 36%).[27] However, other (perhaps less politically charged) causes continue to consistently draw Christians' monetary support despite this shift in attitude.

## Do Local & Global Poverty Compete for Donations?

When forced to choose among hypothetical options for giving, the majority of U.S. adults says they would prefer designating donations for *local* child poverty. A higher proportion in 2017 than in 2003 (23% vs. 7%) says the location of the children being helped "wouldn't matter" to them. Presumably, this group is open to guidance about where an imaginary $100 should go. This change may be related to the reduced proportion who would give to overseas child poverty in 2017 (8% vs. 15%) or to U.S. poverty (64% vs. 74%).

Beyond this hypothetical survey scenario, nothing keeps U.S. adults from giving to multiple issues or the same issue in multiple locations. Survey results show in a few dimensions that practicing Christians particularly do not see fighting poverty as a zero-sum game, where either American or overseas children must lose.

> Practicing Christians do not see fighting poverty as a zero-sum game, where either American or overseas children must lose

**If You Had $100 Set Aside for Child Poverty, Where Would You Donate?**

2003
2017

| Overseas | In the U.S. | Wouldn't matter | Not sure |
| 15% 8% | 74% 64% | 7% 23% | 3% 4% |

2003, *n*=1,000 U.S. adults; May 2017, *n*=1,001 U.S. adults.

In other words, there does *not* seem to be a tradeoff between interest in global poverty and in local poverty. Those who rank global poverty as a priority are more likely to also prioritize local poverty (92%) than those who don't see global poverty as important (74%). In fact, those who say personal action on global poverty is more important are also likely to see *every other* social issue Barna asked about as important, and their actions in giving and service often follow suit.

A motif emerges—one that is foundational to this report, and explored more in the infographic on page 54—that caring about global poverty means caring about other issues. The beautiful reality is that interest and investment in the fight against global poverty cultivate a generous outlook toward many social issues. The more you care, the more you care.

## VOLUNTEERING FOR POVERTY

Over the course of a year, the U.S. Bureau of Labor Statistics finds that a quarter of Americans over 16 years old (25%) volunteers.[28] Along these lines, a January 2017 Barna poll shows that almost a quarter of U.S. adults (23%) reports volunteering at church within the past week, and 29 percent report volunteering to help a nonprofit other than a church.

The likelihood that someone chooses to be a volunteer seems to increase with age, which could be aided by having more opportunity, connections or simply free time as one grows older. This may seem surprising given that the previous chapter illustrated the high levels of compassion and concern among Millennials, but there is some evidence that younger generations' support tends to be more theoretical at this point. (For a typology of poverty mindsets and actions, see page 61.) Senior generations in the Barna

## Activity Types, by Volunteer Levels

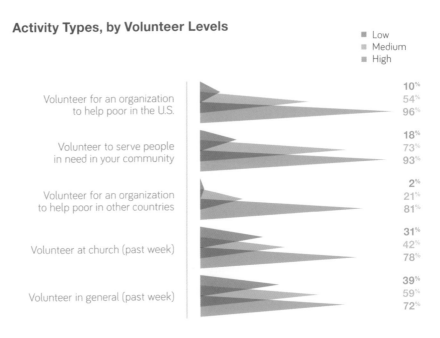

■ Low
■ Medium
■ High

Volunteer for an organization
to help poor in the U.S.

10%
54%
96%

Volunteer to serve people
in need in your community

18%
73%
93%

Volunteer for an organization
to help poor in other countries

2%
21%
81%

Volunteer at church (past week)

31%
42%
78%

Volunteer in general (past week)

39%
59%
72%

May 2017, *n*=1,001 U.S. adults.

poll are more likely than younger ones to volunteer in churches. Three in 10 Boomers (30%) and more than a quarter of Elders (27%) say they volunteer at a church, compared to 16 percent of Millennials and one in five Gen X (21%). This tracks well with Bureau of Labor Statistics data from 2015, which finds Americans ages 35–54 are the most likely age group to volunteer (28%), while Millennials (in that report, a group of adults ages 20-24) are least likely (18% report volunteering the past 12 months).[29]

For this particular study about poverty, Barna asked people a series of questions on volunteering. Analysts categorized these responses to identify various levels of volunteer engagement—high, medium and low—and shed light on the relationship between those who volunteer at all and those who volunteer with the intention of resisting poverty.

Though many American adults volunteer in some capacity, a small, benevolent segment of the population takes on the majority of that work. Barna finds that action against poverty is concentrated among a group of highly active volunteers. Those who are already likely to volunteer are most likely to volunteer with an organization to help the poor in other countries. Highly

Action against poverty is concentrated among a group of highly active volunteers

engaged volunteers account for just one in 10 of all respondents (10%) in the survey—yet they make up 61 percent of those who volunteer for a global organization helping the poor. Looking at it another way, 81 percent of highly engaged volunteers have volunteered for a global organization helping the poor. By comparison, roughly one-fifth of moderately engaged volunteers (21%) and just 2 percent of low-engagement volunteers report the same. There is a healthy link between volunteering to help people in general and showing an active interest in addressing global poverty specifically.

## Volunteering Habits of Christians

Faith affiliation of any kind seems to foster a willingness to give of one's time for charitable causes. Barna finds that adherents of religions other than Christianity are slightly more likely than self-identified Christians and those who do not affiliate with any faith to volunteer. Four in 10 of those of other faiths (40%) volunteer for a non-profit in a given week, compared to one in four Christians (28%) and one-third of those of no faith (32%) who do the same. Looking specifically at volunteering for U.S. poverty, Christians (26%) and other religious people (23%) volunteer at a similar rate, topping that of non-religious adults (18%). This trend continues, though with lower engagement, when addressing global poverty; 15 percent of Christians, 13 percent of those of other faiths and 9 percent of non-religious people have taken part in that type of volunteer work.

A contrast also emerges when dividing all self-identified Christians into practicing and non-practicing groups. Practicing Christians are consistently more generous not only with their money, but with their hours. Weekly volunteering is reported by one in three practicing Christians (33%), compared to 27 percent of non-practicing Christians. About a quarter (24%) has volunteered specifically to combat global poverty, as opposed to one in 10 non-practicing Christians (10%). In their own community, practicing Christians more often report bringing food to a family in need (75% vs. 55% have done so in the past 12 months), directly donating goods other than money to people who are financially poor (72% vs. 61%) and volunteering to help the poor (47% vs. 27%).

This may relate to opportunities that churches provide for volunteering. If practicing Christians are, by definition, spending more time in church, it's reasonable that they'd have more knowledge of local and global needs, as well as chances to participate in projects or campaigns that need volunteers. For

## Weekly Volunteering in Churches

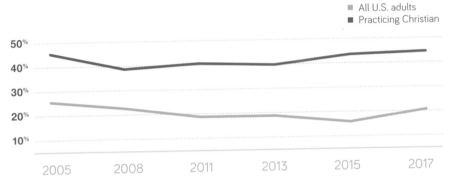

■ All U.S. adults
■ Practicing Christian

2005, *n*=2,006 U.S. adults, 436 practicing Christians; 2008, *n*=1,004 U.S. adults, 476 practicing Christians; 2011, *n*=1,567 U.S. adults, 559 practicing Christians; 2013; *n*=2,036 U.S. adults, 661 practicing Christians; 2015; *n*=806 U.S. adults, 215 practicing Christians; May 2017, *n*=1,001 U.S. adults, 219 practicing Christians.

example, in Barna and Thrivent Financial's study on generosity, 59 percent of Christian churchgoers say their church gave them opportunities to provide services such as meals or building houses.[30]

## Service & Missions Trips

Travel for service projects, such as short-term missions trips, is relatively rare, confirming that Americas' role in global anti-poverty work is still primarily as benefactor. Only 6 percent say they have traveled outside the U.S. to serve the poor or unfortunate in the past year.

A sense of individual responsibility to combat poverty is common among those who have actually gone overseas to serve, suggesting that many of those with this conviction are making a concerted effort to practice what they preach, or that those who have already traveled and seen firsthand the devastating reality of poverty return home with great personal commitment. One-fifth of those who place global poverty in their top three social concerns (20%) and 30 percent of those who believe they can personally have a major impact in poverty alleviation have also served those who are poor abroad. Those who have traveled outside the U.S. to serve the poor or disadvantaged (95%) or volunteered at all for global poverty (89%) are also highly likely to have donated for global poverty.

Despite the seeming emphasis on short-term missions opportunities in and through churches—in a previous Barna study conducted with Thrivent Financial, 40 percent of churchgoing Christians say their churches encourage people to join missions trips[31]—just 10 percent of practicing Christians have embarked on a service trip. Even so, this is still much higher—three times more, in fact—than the percentage of those with no faith who have gone abroad to work against poverty (3%).

## HOW DEMOGRAPHICS AFFECT ENGAGEMENT

Though many U.S. adults are involved in anti-poverty efforts, there are differences in involvement based on ethnicity, income, ideology, gender and more.

Personal prosperity has a mixed effect on an inclination to fight poverty, and prosperity itself is strongly tied to demographics in the U.S. For instance, white Americans have a higher socioeconomic status than black or Hispanic Americans. Men typically earn and own more than women do.[32] Wealthy people are more likely to marry, and married people are wealthier.[33] Boomers are wealthier than Millennials. And, to further complicate the picture, these different factors interact with each other, sometimes mitigating or exaggerating each other's effects.

Generally speaking, the further one is from poverty, the more likely one is to financially address it—even though, as the report previously mentioned, prosperous Americans are less likely to prioritize anti-poverty action. This may be one strong example of how concern and action are not necessarily synonymous. (For more on this practical approach to support, see Barna's poverty action types on page 61.) In

(For more on this practical approach to support, see Barna's poverty action types on page 61.)

### PUT IT TO USE

**Ask**

Pastors, what is your current approach to missions and education experiences for your church? How often does your church provide opportunities to travel and serve the poor? Are you publicly sharing the enthusiasm and insight of those who have participated in such trips?

**Do**

If your ministry hasn't yet, select one church in a poor region to partner with for the long term. This might include not only sending congregants on service trips, but also inviting those partners to visit your church. Group sponsorship of children living in the same area is another way to cultivate a church-wide connection to a single place.

this study, people in the wealthier groups, on average, are more likely to report giving. Do they have some ethical sense that, as Luke 12:48 states, "When someone has been given much, much will be required in return?" It's unclear

## Where Different Ethnicities Direct Their Donations

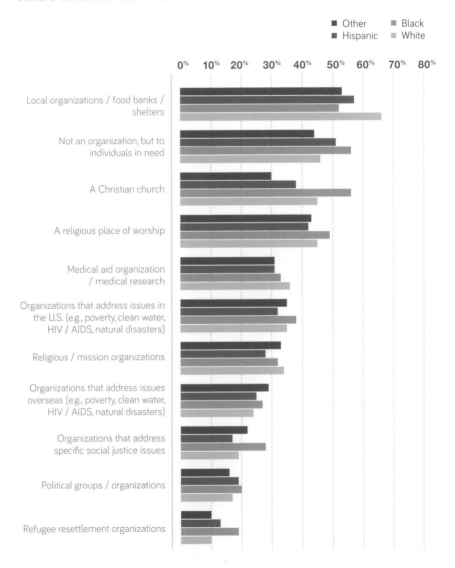

May 2017, *n*=1,001 U.S. adults.

whether having more money enables them to act on long-held generosity or if their giving priorities have altered with their context or increased means.

Socioeconomic status also has some influence on the amount of *time* people give; people with lower incomes—less than $50,000 a year—report lower rates of volunteering than those with higher incomes (63% did not volunteer in the past month, vs. 50% earning $50,000–$99,999 and 48% earning $100,000 or more).

However, this order—of greater wealth and a greater inclination to give and serve—does not hold along some demographic divisions, particularly ethnicity. Notably, black Americans—the least wealthy ethnic group in the U.S.[34]—are more likely than white Americans to donate to individuals in need (56%), churches (56%), social justice issues (28%) and refugee resettlement organizations (19%). It's possible that black Americans, likely more acquainted with poverty themselves, often channel their empathy into action. Indeed, one study found that personal exposure to poverty may inspire personal involvement: People in neighborhoods affected by poverty are more disposed to donating, whether they are poor or wealthy, while wealthy people who live in wealthy neighborhoods are less so.[35] Additionally, various studies have shown that the poorest 20 percent of Americans give relatively more of their income.[36] An up-close, in-person awareness of humanity's needs proves to be a vital catalyst in meeting the needs of others, regardless of one's own resources.

On only one of the donation opportunities listed are white Americans significantly more likely to engage; 66 percent, compared to 54 percent of non-white Americans, have given to local organizations, food banks or shelters. They are equally as likely to

## PUT IT TO USE

### Think

The numbers show that ethnic minorities in the U.S. are some of the most fervent, consistent advocates for the materially poor, in the U.S. and abroad—pointing to yet another reason the Church is strengthened by intentional diversity on leadership teams and in the pews.

### Ask

How often is your church being led by and listening to minority voices? Is your missions work a truly multicultural effort?

# THE MORE YOU CARE, THE MORE YOU CARE

An orientation toward confronting global poverty seems to make people more aware of all sorts of social issues they could help with—and is associated with actually doing something about these causes. Whether concern begets action, or action begets concern, the data suggests an encouraging cycle of engagement and compassion.

## U.S. adults who donate to help children in extreme poverty are also:

- ■ Donors for global poverty
- ■ Those who have not donated for global poverty

### Generous in other areas of their lives

77%
51%

77% have provided food for a needy family

74%
59%

74% have donated in-kind items

53%
20%

53% help their neighbors

48%
15%

48% volunteer to alleviate domestic poverty

28%
7%

28% volunteer for an organization to help the poor in other countries

### Anchored by an active faith

68% are Christians,
45% of whom are practicing Christians

68%
63%

50% have spent time praying for other people

50%
27%

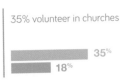

35% volunteer in churches

35%
18%

May 2017, n=1,001 U.S. adults.

## More concerned about a range of issues

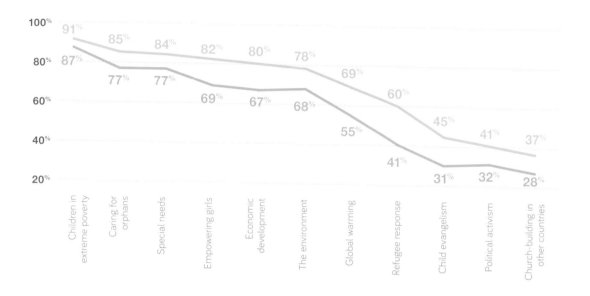

Service trip participation and volunteering are correlated with high concern for poverty and confidence in one's personal influence

**95%** of those who have traveled outside the U.S. to serve the poor

and

**89%** of those who have spent time volunteering for global poverty

have also donated to address child poverty

**1 in 5** of those who place global poverty in their top three social concerns

and

**3 in 10** of those who believe they can have a major influence on global poverty

have also done anti-poverty service work abroad

**Do**

Considering what people tell Barna they'd like to learn about poverty, churches may want to

- distribute fact sheets about the state of poverty
- allow donors and volunteers to publicly reflect on their experiences
- ask an expert to compile ideas for action in a pamphlet or e-book
- share stats, articles or stories about global poverty through social media accounts
- design a spot on the ministry's site devoted to details about the church's impact

give to medical aid / research and religious organizations as non-white Americans.

For most causes, including global poverty or children in extreme poverty, age has little to no impact on an adult's willingness to donate money. Generational engagement does vary, though, on issues that could be seen as spiritually or politically charged, perhaps because of younger generations' increasingly liberal and decreasingly religious affiliation. For instance, Elders favor giving to Christian churches (56% vs. 38% of Millennials), while Millennials are the generation most likely to want to financially support refugee resettlement (20% vs. 5% of Elders).

## WHO DO PEOPLE TRUST ON POVERTY?

The foundation of poverty engagement—before anybody ever donates a dollar, signs up as a volunteer or boards a plane—begins with awareness. On an issue as complex, widespread and urgent as poverty, levels and types of engagement are inevitably linked to the quality of the information people receive about scarcity in the U.S. and abroad. In the first chapter we covered how few Americans have an accurate assessment of current poverty levels, so it's worth asking, from whom or what are they learning? Which individuals, institutions and sources do they look to as leaders on poverty?

When actively seeking information on poverty, U.S. adults start with looking for basic information (71%). More than half (53%) want to know ideas for implementation, while 46 percent are looking for success stories from the field. The practical emphasis continues: 37 percent look for actual resources, and 28 percent hope to find ways to join in. Though only a fifth of all adults (19%) is interested in learning about

## Desired Poverty Information & Resources

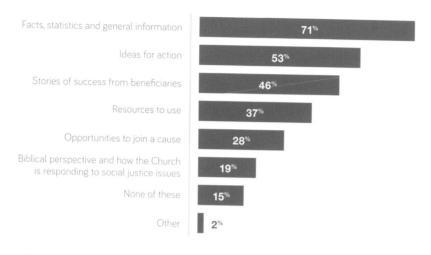

| | |
|---|---|
| Facts, statistics and general information | 71% |
| Ideas for action | 53% |
| Stories of success from beneficiaries | 46% |
| Resources to use | 37% |
| Opportunities to join a cause | 28% |
| Biblical perspective and how the Church is responding to social justice issues | 19% |
| None of these | 15% |
| Other | 2% |

May 2017, n = 1,001 U.S. adults. Respondents were asked to choose their top three desired pieces of information.

a Christian perspective on poverty, evangelicals and practicing Christians are predictably more intrigued by biblical perspectives (59%) and accounts of the Church's actions against poverty so far (45%).

In terms of the sources that people trust, U.S. adults, including practicing Christians, place a high level of trust in those with first-hand experience with poverty. Significant majorities of U.S. adults (89%) and practicing Christians (92%) say they would "definitely" or "probably" give credence to the opinions of someone who has worked in addressing poverty. Equal percentages (88% of U.S. adults; 92% of practicing Christians) would trust someone who has personally lived in and been touched by poverty.

Individuals also play a pivotal role in disseminating their knowledge of or mindsets about poverty within their immediate spheres of influence. Close friends (86%) and family members (83%) have at least some sway with a majority of Americans, including practicing Christians (88% for each), in poverty discussions.

Given that the opinions of more personal connections are clearly so valued, and that Americans now find themselves in an era defined by deinstitutionalization and the "fake news" debate, it's not a shock that public figures pull little trust on the subject of poverty. This includes groups who are

> More than half of U.S. adults want to know how to act on poverty

## U.S. Adults' Most Trusted Sources on Global Poverty

*Thinking about the individual presented below, would you trust his or her opinion when it comes to the issue of global poverty?*

■ Definitely ■ Probably ▪ Probably not ■ Definitely not

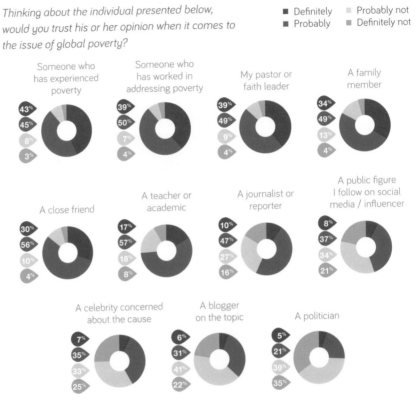

May 2017, *n*=1,001 U.S. adults.

expected to be experts and policy makers, such as reporters and politicians. Nearly three-quarters of U.S. adults (74%) are cautious about politicians' perspectives on global poverty, including more than a third (35%) who "definitely" don't trust them. Though most U.S. adults (57%) still trust a journalist at least somewhat on the topic of global poverty, practicing Christians are less likely to do so; more than half (52%) "probably" or "definitely" don't value reporters' opinions on global poverty. Sadly, this leaves most U.S. adults and Christians mistrusting subject experts, thought leaders and many of the sources who compile broad information on the topic of global poverty. At the same time, Americans are more likely to say they would put at least some level of trust in most sources than not, indicating that there is room for U.S. adults to accept influence.

The opinions of online influencers or entertainers don't carry much weight. A majority of U.S. adults says they do not see bloggers (63% "definitely" + "probably" not), celebrities concerned about the cause (58% "definitely" + "probably" not) or public figures they follow on social media (55% "definitely" + "probably" not) as reputable sources on global poverty. However, this could be an example of the tension between, or at least the ignorance about, what people *say* and what they really *do* or believe. Other research on the most-trusted Americans is, by definition, made up of celebrities and public figures. For instance, actor Tom Hanks has been selected as the most trusted

## Practicing Christians Most Trust Pastors on Global Poverty

*Thinking about the individual presented below, would you trust his or her opinion when it comes to the issue of global poverty?*

■ Definitely     ▨ Probably not
■ Probably       ■ Definitely not

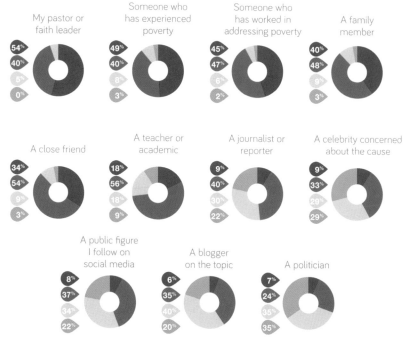

May 2017, *n*=219 practicing Christians.

person in America multiple times.[37] And there's certainly some strategy at work in sending entertainers and artists as goodwill ambassadors to draw attention to poverty around the world.

There is one other figure who inspires high levels of trust, at least on this topic. Among practicing Christians, for whom addressing poverty is inevitably spiritual in nature, the *most* trusted source on global poverty is in turn a spiritual authority: pastors and faith leaders. Almost all practicing Christians (94%) probably or definitely value their own pastors' thoughts about global poverty. Evangelicals are particularly trusting; nearly two-thirds (64%) place total confidence in what their pastor has to say about global poverty.

Perhaps this has to do with how much the Bible itself says about poverty; Compassion International identifies more than 2,000 references in the Bible to children, poverty and compassion, which likely make their way into Sunday sermons.[38] But a relationship to scripture or church attendance isn't even required to have faith in pastors on this subject: Among all U.S. adults, pastors are the most trusted source concerning the world's poor, tied with those who have worked or lived in a poverty environment.

In the next chapter, the data introduces us to the ardent, yet somewhat uncertain, spiritual leaders of the global poverty fight.

Pastors are the most trusted source concerning the world's poor, tied with those who have worked or lived in a poverty environment

# THE POVERTY ACTION TYPES

Combinations of theory and practice in global poverty engagement

There is a befuddling gap between the public's aspiration and action. Though this is sometimes correlated to the income, resources or connections at an individual's disposal, other factors are also at work. In an effort to examine how various approaches to poverty are formed and persist, Barna identified four types of respondents, grouped by their sense of personal responsibility to address global poverty and their level of support of anti-poverty work.

**Responsive Supporters**
- consider global poverty to be more important to personally support through personal donations and volunteering
- have given more than $50 to address global poverty in the past year

**Uninvolved**
- consider global poverty to be less important to personally support through personal donations and volunteering
- have not given more than $50 to address global poverty in the past year

25%

33%

28%

14%

**Practical Supporters**
- consider global poverty to be less important to personally support through personal donations and volunteering
- have given more than $50 to address global poverty in the past year

**Theoretical Supporters**
- consider global poverty to be more important to personally support through personal donations and volunteering
- have not given more than $50 to address global poverty in the past year

May 2017, n=1,001 U.S. adults.

## Uninvolved

Unfortunately, the plurality of respondents (33%) qualifies as what Barna refers to as **Uninvolved**—those who have neither given money ($50 or more in the past year) to combat global poverty nor feel it is important to be personally involved in such efforts. Four of five people in this group (80%) did not give any money for global poverty in the past year. About half (52%) donated toward domestic poverty.

This group, predominantly Boomers (36%) and Gen X (33%), cares less and does less. On no issue included in the survey did they indicate more inclination than the other types to get personally involved, so it's no surprise that 7 in 10 (69%) have not volunteered in the past month. Uninvolved adults are less likely to believe it is important for them to help with child poverty (77%), child trafficking (75%), local poverty (70%) and economic development in poor countries (50%). This group tends toward conservative (39%) or moderate (45%) ideology. Nearly a fifth of the Uninvolved (17%) is uninspired by the idea of ending poverty in 25 years.

These individuals are inclined to shift responsibility for the world's poor onto others (50% say it's "mostly" or "entirely" someone else's job) and are the type most likely to expect the government of a poor nation to deal with it (49%). It's possible that a lack of interest in global poverty is associated with a sense of powerlessness to address the issue.

Though a majority (61%) is Christian, this group is less religious than the others, with more than a quarter (26%) saying they have no religion and, of the Christians, most are not practicing (73%). Christians who are Uninvolved don't regard the involvement or financial investment of the Church as absolutely critical to the cause of poverty, and just more than one in five (22%) sees anti-poverty work as an avenue to better understand the heart of Christ. It makes sense then, that these believers are also very unlikely (10%) to see their lack of care for the poor and vulnerable as a reflection on their Christianity.

## Theoretical Supporters

Unlike the Uninvolved, the next group actually prioritizes personal involvement on global poverty—but in theory only. **Theoretical Supporters**, which make up 28 percent of the sample, are not very likely to spend time or money, even on this issue that they say is important to them. The engagement of this group, often taken up by liberal (36%) or moderate (39%) individuals, could probably be likened to what is now commonly called "slacktivism." This stereotype is usually applied to Millennials, and they indeed are the most represented age group (40%). Similar percentages of Theoretical Supporters have neither donated to help children in extreme poverty in the last year (71%) nor volunteered in the past month (72%). Of those who did donate something, two-thirds (66%) donated $20 or less. Theoretical Supporters' giving for domestic poverty (45%) mirrors that of the Uninvolved. However, it should be noted that some of this group may be held back not by apathy but by a lower income—37 percent earn less than $30,000 annually, as opposed to the Uninvolved who are spread a little more widely across tax brackets.

Also like the Uninvolved, they primarily assign poor nations with the responsibility for global poverty (40%), though more than a third (34%) says international non-profits have a key role to play. These respondents tend to be less religious (24% are "nones," 58% are Christians, 29% are practicing Christians) than the groups who donate more money.

Their lack of embodied concern is even more unfortunate given that more than half of the Christians in this group (53%) believe that aiding the poor could draw people into a deeper understanding of Christ. Less than a quarter (24%) has read an article about the plight of the poor in the past three months, though 58 percent would at least like a better grasp of biblical ideas about poverty.

## Practical Supporters

Perhaps the most interesting donor group are those who gave at least $50 to address child poverty over the year, but also say they do *not* feel

### Poverty Action Types & Personal Responsibility

"Ending poverty in 25 years feels like ..."

- Responsive Supporters
- Theoretical Supporters
- Practical Supporters
- Uninvolved

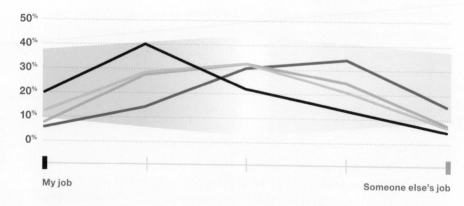

May 2017, *n*=1,001 U.S. adults.

personally called to act against global poverty: **Practical Supporters**. They tend to split the responsibility for global poverty between foreign governments (36%) and international non-profits (28%). Their interest may be more practical and less sentimental, or perhaps their involvement is simply connected to a broader obligation to address needs, rather than an overt concern for poverty. Although the data doesn't say much about *when* people give, other research suggests reasons people might donate to causes they don't believe are essential. Context matters, and many good behaviors (as well as bad ones) are contagious. For example, people tend to give more money when peers with whom they identify in some important way are also giving money.[39]

As the wealthiest of the poverty action types (39% make more than $75,000 annually), it's possible this group is often called on to help with funding; they stick to what they do best, while giving generously of their finances and leaving the "work" of reducing poverty to the experts. Fittingly, although many do find time to volunteer for local causes, they are more in sync with Theoretical Supporters when it comes to volunteering for the global poor specifically (11%).

More than four in 10 among this segment (44%) are Boomers, conservatives (40%) or moderates (41%). They donate an average of $673 to children in extreme poverty annually. This smallest of groups (14% of respondents) is also most likely to donate to local organizations, food banks and shelters; a large majority (87%) has.

Practical Supporters are on the religious side; 79 percent are Christians, the highest proportion of all the groups, and more than half (57%) have been to church in the past month. It could be that this faithful group acts on "sacred values."[40] This isn't to say people never violate sacred values, but when they do so, it is uncomfortable. So if a Christian believes that God wants her to give to the poor, she may not need any other reason to do so. Christians who are Practical Supporters could be further activated in this spiritual, emotional sense; more than half (53%) are at least somewhat interested in learning more about scriptural insights on poverty, and 62 percent ("very" + "somewhat" interested) would like to know how churches should respond to social justice issues. A healthy proportion (44%) thinks that poverty engagement results in a deeper understanding of Christ.

## Poverty Action Types & Personal Influence

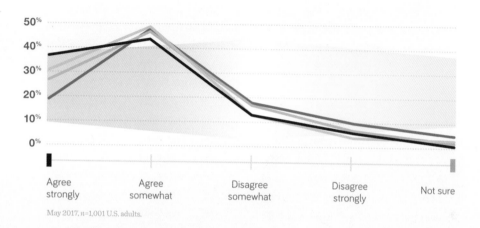

"One person can really make a difference in solving poverty for one child"

- ■ Responsive Supporters
- ■ Theoretical Supporters
- ■ Practical Supporters
- ■ Uninvolved

50%
40%
30%
20%
10%
0%

Agree strongly    Agree somewhat    Disagree somewhat    Disagree strongly    Not sure

May 2017, *n*=1,001 U.S. adults.

## Responsive Supporters

Occasionally, people exhibit an emotional response to poverty *and* back it up with practical action. This group sees their personal involvement as important, and thus they choose to donate (an amount of at least $50 in the past year). **Responsive Supporters** make up a quarter of respondents (24%). Overall, they give an average amount of $1,362 to children in extreme poverty annually. In keeping with a theme of Barna's study—that a general level of concern or action translates to multiple causes—both Responsive and Practical Supporters also donate to domestic poverty at a higher rate than Theoretical Supporters and Uninvolved adults. Six in 10 Responsive Supporters (61%) give toward this issue.

Responsive Supporters are the only type to primarily task international non-profits with handling global poverty (32%), though one in 10 says individual donors should take the lead (10%), more than any other group of supporters. The Responsive group feels a heavy responsibility for ending poverty; one in five (20%) indicates that ending poverty in 25 years is entirely their job, and another 41 percent accept most of the responsibility. Even beyond donations, their habits reflect this conviction; Responsive Supporters are the most active participants in all actions included in the survey, including volunteering to help the poor, whether in the U.S. (48%) or overseas (30%).

More often than not, these compassionate adults are from the Gen X (40%) or Millennial (33%) generations. Responsive Supporters are more evenly distributed by ideology than any of the other action types (38% liberal, 31% conservative, 31% moderate), pointing to some encouraging common ground in political camps.

Responsive Supporters' activism and optimism appear to bolster each other; they are the group most likely to believe that one person can really make a difference in solving poverty for one child (81% agree at least somewhat) and that ending global poverty in the next 25 years feels possible (63%) or believable (62%). Whole-hearted engagement may depend on a balance of both concern and hope for a particular issue.

It's possible that religious conviction compels some of their activity; two-thirds of Responsive Supporters (67%) are Christians, and 43 percent are practicing Christians, the highest number among the poverty action types. They are the most active church attenders (68% have been to church in the past month). A majority of these Christians believes that helping the poor in turn helps Christians understand the heart of Christ (58%) and has spent significant time praying for the poor (53%). Forty-four percent of Responsive Christians say that their churches should prioritize spending resources to address poverty in other countries. Christians in this group are also the most eager for information on poverty; eight in 10 are at least somewhat interested in learning more about a biblical perspective on poverty (79%) or hearing about how the Church could be involved (80%).

Christians in both the Responsive and Practical Supporter categories are similarly likely to give to missions organizations (50% and 53%, respectively) and to their churches (59% and 64%, respectively). The same goes for Christians who are Uninvolved or Theoretical Supporters, though in lesser proportions (20% and 21% have given to missions and 33% and 34% have given to churches, respectively). This suggests that there is not a tradeoff between Christian donations toward global poverty and donations to missions—and perhaps undermines a common argument that Christians might hold back on fighting poverty because they first want to address spiritual or evangelistic needs.

## Poverty Types & Perceptions of Global Poverty Fight

"Ending poverty in 25 years feels ... "

- ■ Responsive Supporters
- ■ Theoretical Supporters
- ■ Practical Supporters
- ■ Uninvolved

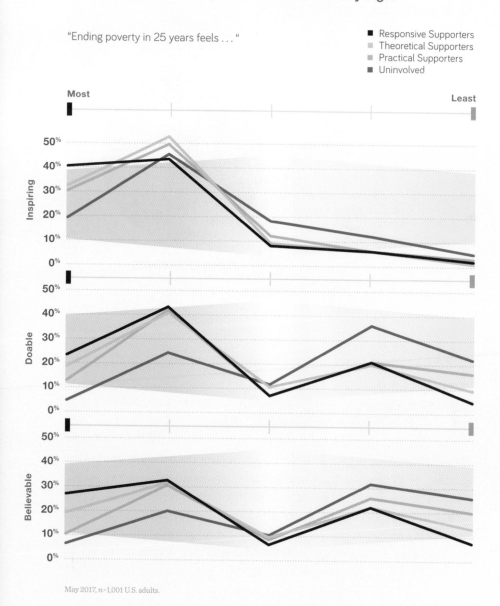

May 2017, n=1,001 U.S. adults.

# THE POWER OF PERSONAL GIVING

## Q&A WITH JOHN CORTINES

John serves as chief operating officer at Generous Giving, a non-profit that seeks to spread the biblical message of generosity. He holds an MBA from Harvard Business School and speaks regularly at large churches and conferences around the country. He is co-author of the book *God and Money*. John and his wife, Megan, have three children and reside in Orlando, Florida.

**JOHN CORTINES**
Author, COO of Generous Giving

Q What are some ways that the Church or Christians in community can foster transparency and accountability—for the individual, and the collective—in their giving to help the poor?

We want our giving to have an impact, and we want the dollars to be used the way they were intended. Thus, any church or non-profit has a duty to pursue audits of their finances and results, and to study the efficacy of their programs. Conducting and sharing the results of evidence-based research studies that quantify the impact of programs is a highly commendable step. It should be easy for any program donor to understand that 1) their dollars will go where they intend them to and 2) the organization studies impact and diligently seeks to improve their results over time.

Beyond this, anecdotal stories of impact that put a human face on the statistics are hugely important. I've heard it said, "Never share a statistic without a story, and never share a story without a statistic." We need to see the human elements of a single story, and we need to understand the big-picture, macro-level impact. They go hand-in-hand.

Q What are some ways you might encourage a more relational connection for the altruistic, often wealthier Practical Supporters, or a more tangible effort among the sympathetic Theoretical group who struggle to get involved?

I hear two things all the time: First, people say, "Wow, I never knew the Bible said so much about poverty and about helping the poor." Exposure to God's Word on this subject is a major motivator for Christians. Because this is not a popular subject from the pulpit, people tend to not know how big of a deal poverty is to God!

Secondly, people also say, "I want to help the poor, but I don't really know any poor people." They fail to bridge the gap between their desire to give and the opportunity to fund a highly efficient global non-profit.

Thus, people would benefit from 1) a deeper understanding of God's heart for the poor and 2) exposure to the easy opportunity to give to those in extreme poverty through a major non-profit organization. These steps have to be sequential, in my estimation. Exposure to a giving opportunity doesn't inspire action unless someone first understands how much God cares about this subject. Biblical understanding comes first, then the opportunity to give can follow.

"We need to see the human elements of a single story, and we need to understand the big-picture, macro-level impact."

# THE PSYCHOLOGY BEHIND GIVING DECISIONS

By Susan Mettes

Who doesn't have clean water? Usually, someone who is materially poor and lives where the government doesn't provide many services. In all likelihood, people without clean water have an array of other problems related to poverty. So, why are U.S. adults in this Barna survey more inclined to support clean water initiatives than global poverty alleviation? It may have more to do with human psychology, rather than a lack of concern for the sweeping issue of global poverty. Let's look at a few factors that research shows often impact decision-making and giving.

## Specificity Motivates

Whether or not they know it, the choosy potential donors in this survey may be following some good advice on reaching a big, general, long-term goal. One of the practical applications to come out of decades of research on motivation is SMART goals.[41] SMART goals are **s**pecific, **m**easurable, **a**ttainable, **r**ealistic and **t**ime-specific. The Millennium Development Goals, for example, abide by these standards.

One of these goals was to "halve, between 1990 and 2015, the proportion of people whose income is less than $1 a day." And we did it—five years ahead of schedule.[42] Now, many charities are working on the Sustainable Development Goals, which call for eradicating extreme poverty everywhere by 2030.[43]

Cutting big problems down into smaller, more specific problems can be very helpful.[44] Contributing to clean water or literacy may make you feel like you're tackling a smart (or SMART) goal—something easier to grasp and more motivating than the general idea of fighting global poverty.

## The Catalyst of Individual Connections

Our brains also seem wired to want to help more when the act might affect most if not all of the victims.[45] This is one component of what researchers have come to call the "identifiable victim effect."[46] When we see an individual suffering—and especially if we believe that individual is not responsible for their bad situation—we are more likely

"Cutting big problems down into smaller, more specific problems can be very helpful."

to respond than if we hear about a large, somewhat impersonal grouping of people affected.[47] When there's a tradeoff, people often choose identifiable victims over statistical victims.[48] Statistical victims register more like numbers in our brains, regardless of how widespread or severe their circumstances may be. In his 1968 article introducing the identifiable victim effect, Thomas Schelling wrote that an individual's death causes "anxiety and sentiment, guilt and awe, responsibility and religion, [but]. . . most of this awesomeness disappears when we deal with statistical death."[49]

Of course, to identify a victim may require personal exposure to a problem. In a study that showed that people in poor neighborhoods donate relatively more, the identifiable victim effect (and maybe much more) is at play.[50]

I now live in Burundi, a country where a high percentage of people are extremely poor, and can attest to the power of personal engagement with those touched by poverty. It would be hard *not* to think of my neighbors when deciding about charity donations in the future.

## A Tendency to Normalize

But, history has taught us, exposure to poverty is not all that counts. After all, even a high proportion of dictators comes from humble origins. And we all can likely name someone who sees suffering and blames the victim—or just doesn't notice. Why does this happen? In part, it is because every human is in danger of getting used to things they should not get used to. This is the psychological principle known as the "hedonic treadmill"—basically, the idea that we acclimate to nearly everything after a while and return to a normal emotional state.[51] This can be a benefit when recovering from job loss, disabilities or other big problems—but on the other hand, it can also make us callous to the trauma or trials of others.

For some reason, being human means caring about **specific victims** and **specific goals**. If only those impulses were more strategic! We might reduce poverty more if statistics played on our heartstrings, too. I don't necessarily believe that impulses like the identifiable victim effect are tendencies we should resist in the name of efficiency; scripture tells us that Jesus also felt the waves of compassion when personally and specifically confronted with needs (see Matthew 9:36, Matthew 14:14 or Luke 7:13). And, after all, it's the Creator, not any individual, who can fully bear the weight of all the pain *and* all the statistics in the world. But there is something we should resist: getting used to poverty, near or far.

## SUSAN METTES
Research analyst

Susan holds degrees from Northwestern University (BA) and Duke University (MPP). She is an editor-at-large for *Christianity Today* magazine, after having worked there as international editor from 2006–2009. Her work history includes positions at Thrivent Financial and Duke University, where she researched topics such as behavioral economics and church life. She has done writing and research for the Barna Group, Gates Foundation, World Vision and Dan Ariely at the Center for Advanced Hindsight. Currently, she lives in Burundi with her husband.

# THE PASTOR'S ROLE

## A PEP TALK FOR THE SPIRITUAL LEADERS
## OF ANTI-POVERTY WORK

How do pastors currently perceive and steward their decisive influence on the subject of poverty—a life-saving responsibility?

In some ways, the trust that the American public places in pastors' opinions of poverty presents an increasingly rare public platform for ministers: Barna research in partnership with Pepperdine University underscores a sort of "cultural credibility crisis" for pastors, showing that just one in five U.S. adults sees Christian clergy as very influential in their community (19%) or as an esteemed voice on important issues of our day (21%).[52] Yet pastors have incredible potential to lead the charge and position the U.S. Church as a powerful force in anti-poverty endeavors—whether they like it or not.

If you ask most pastors, ending global poverty is a nice idea—and out of reach. Half, on average, believe that one person could make a difference in solving poverty for one child. Though a similar proportion also finds the goal of ending poverty in 25 years "inspirational," they are less likely than practicing Christians to find it "believable" or "doable" as well. It's possible that some church leaders, correctly sensing their commission to confront poverty, feel pressured and ill-equipped to do so.

## GAUGING SOCIAL INFLUENCE

Pastors offer a modest assessment of their own potential impact on many social concerns. The cause for which pastors are most likely to assume the highest degree of influence is child evangelism (37% "major"). This makes sense, given that it certainly plays to most pastors' strengths of teaching and discipleship, but pastors also indicate elsewhere in the survey that they feel their personal involvement is important in multiple causes related to vulnerable children (34% child evangelism, 31% child trafficking, 27% orphan care, 25% child poverty).

A majority says they could have at least "some," if not a "major" influence on local poverty (83%), disaster response (76%), caring for orphans (72%),

> Pastors have incredible potential to lead the charge and position the U.S. Church as a powerful force in anti-poverty endeavors—whether they like it or not

## Pastors' Most Important Issues to Be Involved in, Compared to Practicing Christians'

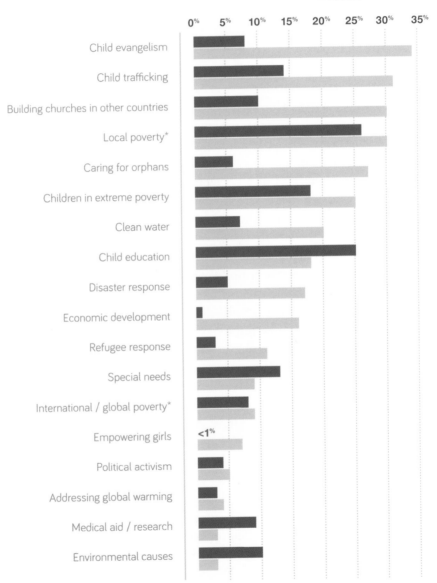

May 2017, *n*=609 pastors, 219 practicing Christians.

*The broader categories of "international / global poverty" and "local poverty" were presented here neutrally, alongside other issues and causes that could rightfully be categorized as aspects of poverty action.

education for disadvantaged children (66%), child poverty (64%), clean water (61%), building churches abroad (60%), special needs (60%) or child trafficking (54%).

Less often, pastors feel comfortable exercising influence on issues of policy, which could be linked to party-line pressures, religious liberty concerns

## Pastors: Ending Poverty in 25 Years Is …

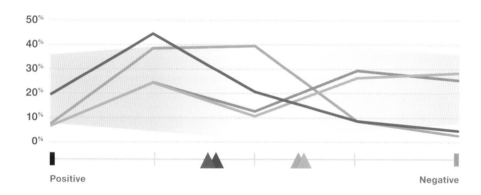

- ■ Inspiring / Uninspiring
- ■ Believable / Not believable
- ■ Doable / Not doable
- ■ My job / Someone else's job

▲ Mean

Positive                                                    Negative

May 2017, n=609 pastors.

## Pastors: "One Person Can Really Make a Difference in Solving Poverty for One Child"

6% 2% 1%

48%

44%

- ■ Agree strongly
- ■ Agree somewhat
- ■ Disagree somewhat
- ■ Disagree strongly
- ■ Don't know

May 2017, n=609 pastors.

## Pastors' Sense of Influence on Various Causes

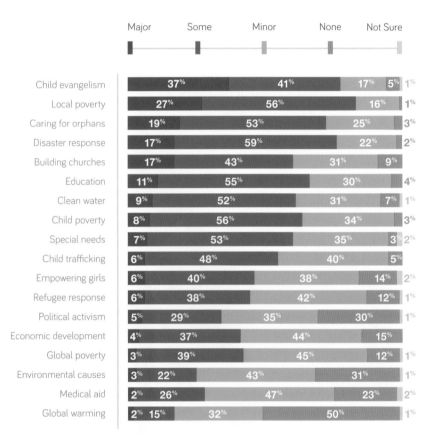

| | Major | Some | Minor | None | Not Sure |
|---|---|---|---|---|---|
| Child evangelism | 37% | 41% | 17% | 5% | 1% |
| Local poverty | 27% | 56% | 16% | | 1% |
| Caring for orphans | 19% | 53% | 25% | | 3% |
| Disaster response | 17% | 59% | 22% | | 2% |
| Building churches | 17% | 43% | 31% | 9% | |
| Education | 11% | 55% | 30% | | 4% |
| Clean water | 9% | 52% | 31% | 7% | 1% |
| Child poverty | 8% | 56% | 34% | | 3% |
| Special needs | 7% | 53% | 35% | 3% | 2% |
| Child trafficking | 6% | 48% | 40% | 5% | |
| Empowering girls | 6% | 40% | 38% | 14% | 2% |
| Refugee response | 6% | 38% | 42% | 12% | 1% |
| Political activism | 5% | 29% | 35% | 30% | 1% |
| Economic development | 4% | 37% | 44% | 15% | |
| Global poverty | 3% | 39% | 45% | 12% | 1% |
| Environmental causes | 3% | 22% | 43% | 31% | 1% |
| Medical aid | 2% | 26% | 47% | 23% | 2% |
| Global warming | 2% | 15% | 32% | 50% | 1% |

May 2017, *n*=609 pastors.

## Ways Pastors Have Shared About Poverty
*(in the past three months)*

**52%**

Discussed poverty with their children, grandchildren or other children they know well

**43%**

Tried to persuade someone else to give of their time or resources to help the global poor

**30%**

Posted content about poverty online to Facebook or other forms of social media

May 2017, *n*=609 pastors.

or simply a lack of interest. Three in 10 senior pastors (30%) feel that they have no influence on political activism anyway. Half (50%) don't feel they have any contribution to make on the highly partisan topic of global warming, and 31 percent say they have no influence on environmental issues in general.

Pastors do sometimes use their position beyond the pulpit to convince others to take action or to think differently about poverty. In the past three months, more than half of the senior pastors in this study (52%) say they spoke with their children, grandchildren or other youths they know well about poverty. Forty-three percent of senior pastors tried to persuade someone to give time or resources to help the poor. Three in 10 (30%) have posted about poverty on social media. For each of these actions, the likelihood that a pastor will speak up increases if they have a high level of concern about poverty, view poverty as their / the Church's responsibility or see ending global poverty as a pragmatic outcome.

## PASTORS ADVOCATE FOR SPIRITUAL SOLUTIONS

A plurality of pastors says the primary responsibility for global poverty falls on humanitarian and non-profit organizations (30%), but they own that churches aren't far behind, placing them as the second-most responsible (26%). Given this close ranking, many pastors may be inclined to see the value in partnering their church with organizations on the ground. Another one in five (19%) says the government of an impoverished nation needs to lead in caring for its own poor.

Pastors see domestic poverty, however, as firmly within the American Church's purview. Perhaps because of the local context and emphasis of most pastoral functions, as well as ministers' awareness

## Pastors: Who Has Primary Responsibility for Global Poverty?

- Businesses
- International non-profit organizations
- The nation's government
- Individual citizens
- Local non-profit organizations
- Churches / places of worship
- Individuals donating to non-profits
- None of the above

## Pastors: Who Has Primary Responsibility for U.S. Poverty?

- Businesses
- Humanitarian and non-profit organizations
- The federal government
- Individual citizens
- State and local governments
- Churches / places of worship

May 2017, *n*=609 pastors.

of and connection to the needs of their immediate rather than international community, fully one-third of pastors (34%) says places of worship bear primary responsibility for the poor in the U.S.

Though pastors more confidently take ownership of local poverty, an equal percentage of pastors in 2008 and 2017 (88% and 86%, respectively) says it's important for Christians in their churches to spend resources on poverty in other countries "given all of the challenges facing the world and this country." When asked how important it is to give to alleviate global poverty, pastors task the Christian community: One in four (24%) believes it's absolutely critical for U.S. churches to offer monetary support. By a few percentage points on average, they assign more importance to the role of U.S. churches collectively than to individual Christians in financially fighting poverty (19%). Unsurprisingly, pastors who feel churches should primarily take on overseas poverty expect more of both (33% churches, 25% individual Christians) than other pastors do.

Considering the nature of their work and calling, pastors place a unique spiritual emphasis on the poverty fight. Just over a third (34%) sees

## Pastors: How Important Is It for Christians or Churches to Give to Alleviate Poverty in Poor Countries?

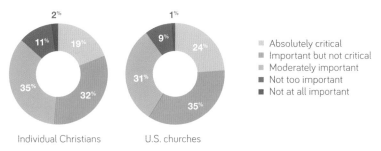

Individual Christians
- 2%
- 11%
- 19%
- 35%
- 32%

U.S. churches
- 1%
- 9%
- 24%
- 31%
- 35%

- Absolutely critical
- Important but not critical
- Moderately important
- Not too important
- Not at all important

May 2017, n=609 pastors.

cultivating spiritual well-being as *the* most effective way to lift people out of poverty, ahead of education (24%) and political change (20%). If a pastor believes churches ultimately answer for global poverty, they are even more likely to look for a spiritual solution to poverty (52%).

This faith-based strategy could be a way for pastors to leverage what they do best in working against poverty, but it may also stem from pastors' familiarity with scriptural remarks about the poor and a strong sense that Christianity both meets our spiritual needs and in turn requires Christians to meet other needs. Pastors may also see the essence of poverty itself as spiritual—the fallout of a "fallen world" and its oppression and greed—thus requiring a response from the righteous. About two-thirds of pastors (65%) agree strongly that helping the poor will draw Christians to a closer understanding of Jesus, and that the Bible teaches that Christians should help children living in poverty (63%). For the latter conviction, the percentage climbs to 69 percent among pastors whose churches donate to anti-poverty efforts.

However, pastors today are generally less likely to emphasize the connection between Christian faith and helping the poor than they were in 2008. In 2008, three of four pastors (75%) strongly agreed that the Bible mandates helping poor children, 8 percentage points more than pastors in 2017. Similarly, there has been an 18-percentage-point drop, from 83 percent, among pastors who strongly affirm that anti-poverty work deepens Christians' relationship to Christ.

Pastors, like congregants, are generally less adamant about the stronger statement that "if Christians are not helping the poor and vulnerable, then

Over a third of pastors sees cultivating spiritual wellbeing as *the* most effective way to lift people out of poverty

they are not true Christians." Elder pastors are particularly lenient on this point; more than half (55%) strongly *disagree* that caring for the poor should be a benchmark of sincere faith (vs. 16% of pastors on average). Female

## How Pastors Link Christianity to Poverty Engagement

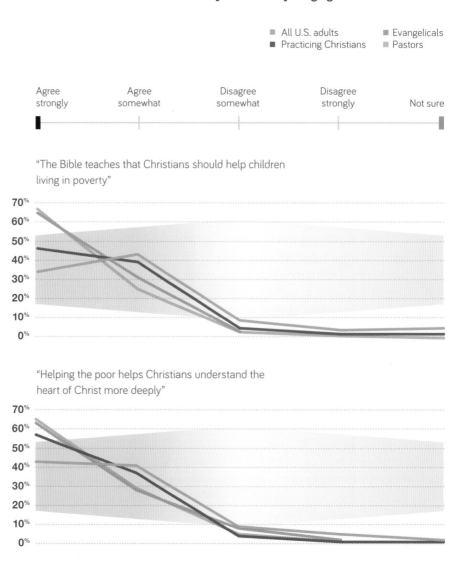

■ All U.S. adults     ■ Evangelicals
■ Practicing Christians     ■ Pastors

| Agree strongly | Agree somewhat | Disagree somewhat | Disagree strongly | Not sure |

"The Bible teaches that Christians should help children living in poverty"

"Helping the poor helps Christians understand the heart of Christ more deeply"

May 2017, *n*=1,001 U.S. adults, *n*=609 pastors.

pastors (44%), leaders who are extremely concerned about the poor (36%) and pastors who speak often on poverty (30%) are among those who strongly believe the integrity of one's faith hinges on their generosity toward those in need. Being able to meet this standard could be incentive to accept it; pastors whose churches already give to address poverty are twice as likely as non-donors to fully agree (22% vs. 9%).

## REPORTS OF ANTI-POVERTY EFFORTS

Consistent with pastors' general belief that churches should be the overseers of anti-poverty work, many of them report this as a concentration in their ministries.

Four of five pastors (84%) say their churches give money specifically to address poverty—a healthy majority, though still a 7-percentage-point drop from nine years ago. Of churches that give toward poverty, one in four (24%) designates half or more of those funds for global poverty. This type of financial generosity is the rule among pastors who are personally worried about the world's poor (94%). Two-thirds of pastors (66%) have also encouraged individuals to give of their own money to combat global poverty. From the pew's perspective, according to a separate study of generosity with Thrivent Financial, more than half of Christian churchgoers (53%) say their churches provide attendees the opportunity to give to organizations.[53] Generally, however, church attendees seem to be less aware of the many chances for engagement that pastors report providing.

Among churches investing in anti-poverty endeavors, the actual amount given annually covers a broad range; on the higher end, 37 percent gave $7,500 or more, while more than a third gave less than $2,500 (36%). Another quarter (26%) falls somewhere in the middle. Logically, larger churches have a little extra room to be generous: Among pastors with congregations of 250 or more people, more than two-thirds (68%) report their giving exceeded $7,500, compared to almost a fifth in small churches (18% of congregations with fewer than 100 people) who report this level of financial commitment.

Pastors point to an array of creative or interactive ways their churches have helped present the cause of poverty to congregants and community. About a third of churches has hosted an event to bring awareness to global poverty (33%), invited a speaker to talk to the congregation about poverty (35%) or held a fundraising campaign for global poverty (37%). More than half of pastors (53%) say their church has planned or hosted a missions trip.

Four of five pastors say their churches give money specifically to address poverty

## Pastors: Did Your Church Donate to Address Poverty Last Year?

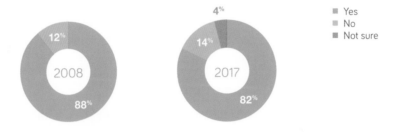

- Yes
- No
- Not sure

2008: 88% Yes, 12% No
2017: 82% Yes, 14% No, 4% Not sure

2008, *n*=503 pastors; May 2017, *n*=609 pastors.

## Pastors and Churchgoers Report on Main Opportunities to Give in Church

- Pastors
- Churchgoers

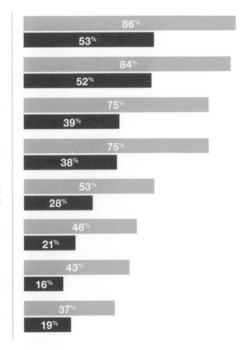

| | Pastors | Churchgoers |
|---|---|---|
| Special offerings of food, goods or money to charitable / non-profit / local organization | 86% | 53% |
| Special offerings for your church's activities or ministries | 84% | 52% |
| Special offerings to overseas missionaries | 75% | 39% |
| Special offerings for crises or natural disasters around the world | 75% | 38% |
| Love offerings or other special offerings for pastors | 53% | 28% |
| Other organized giving | 46% | 21% |
| Church members often initiate their own opportunities to give financially to others | 43% | 16% |
| Child sponsorship | 37% | 19% |

2016, *n*=1,928 Christians who go to church at least annually, 606 U.S. pastors. In partnership with Thrivent Financial.

Pastors also seem to understand that it's important to link arms with existing efforts and experts: A majority of ministries (79%) partners with some kind of non-profit that fights poverty.

A church's size inevitably makes a difference in what a ministry can provide, as most activities and efforts require intentional allocation of ministry resources, volunteers, administration and / or money. Pastors of churches of

## Churches' Activities to Fight Poverty in Past Year, by Church Size

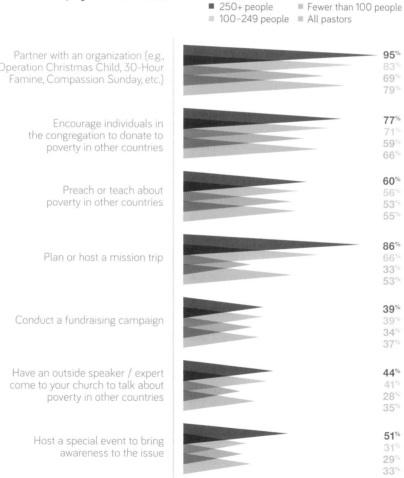

■ 250+ people　　■ Fewer than 100 people
■ 100–249 people　■ All pastors

**Partner with an organization (e.g., Operation Christmas Child, 30-Hour Famine, Compassion Sunday, etc.)**
95%
83%
69%
79%

**Encourage individuals in the congregation to donate to poverty in other countries**
77%
71%
59%
66%

**Preach or teach about poverty in other countries**
60%
56%
53%
55%

**Plan or host a mission trip**
86%
66%
33%
53%

**Conduct a fundraising campaign**
39%
39%
34%
37%

**Have an outside speaker / expert come to your church to talk about poverty in other countries**
44%
41%
28%
35%

**Host a special event to bring awareness to the issue**
51%
31%
29%
33%

May 2017, n=609 pastors.

### Number of Times Pastors Taught on a Christian Response to Poverty, by Poverty Budget

*(in the past year)*

■ None  ■ 2
■ 1  ■ 3 or more

Less than $2,500        $2,500–$7,499        $7,500 or more

May 2017, *n*=609 pastors.

over 250 people tend to have more margin for labor-intensive anti-poverty activities, like hosting a missions trip (86%). Congregations of between 100 and 250 people are still twice as likely to have planned or hosted a missions trip compared to churches of fewer than 100 people (66% and 33%, respectively).

> There is some correlation between pastors using their voices and churches using their funds to address poverty

There is some correlation between pastors using their voices and churches using their funds to address poverty, suggesting pastors set the tone for their church's involvement. Consider that roughly half of all U.S. pastors (55%) report preaching on poverty, yet, in churches with a budget exceeding $7,500 for combating poverty, 79 percent of senior pastors have spoken about a Christian approach to poverty. Thirty-nine percent indicate this happens three or more times a year. Churches with a lower budget for addressing poverty ($2,500 or less) are far less likely to hear about a Christian charge to care for the poor; about half of those pastors (52%) report teaching or preaching about poverty. It's unclear whether a pastor might be compelled to publicly affirm the investments of their church, or whether a church's funds might follow the passions of its leadership, only that influence and finances tend to synchronize.

## Evaluations of Church Involvement

When reporting on their church's involvement with various social issues, pastors' responses mostly reflect their own priorities or the causes in which they assume a certain amount of impact. Local poverty (33% "very involved") and child evangelism (29% "very involved") again feature prominently. More than half of pastors say that their churches are at least somewhat involved in disaster response and child poverty (both 53%). Orphan care, church-building, education, global poverty and special needs are other common church initiatives. Three-quarters of pastors say their churches aren't too concerned with environmental work (72%) or global warming (81%), some of the same politicized issues frequently avoided by pastors and Christians in Barna's survey.

As you might expect, it's an incredibly unpopular idea among pastors, or any circle, for that matter, that a church should be *less* involved in global

## Pastors: How Involved Is Your Church in Each of the Following Social Issues?

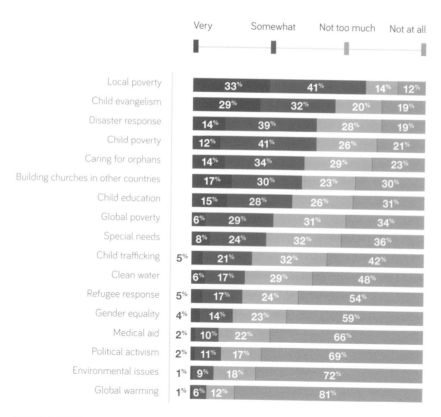

| | Very | Somewhat | Not too much | Not at all |
|---|---|---|---|---|
| Local poverty | 33% | 41% | 14% | 12% |
| Child evangelism | 29% | 32% | 20% | 19% |
| Disaster response | 14% | 39% | 28% | 19% |
| Child poverty | 12% | 41% | 26% | 21% |
| Caring for orphans | 14% | 34% | 29% | 23% |
| Building churches in other countries | 17% | 30% | 23% | 30% |
| Child education | 15% | 28% | 26% | 31% |
| Global poverty | 6% | 29% | 31% | 34% |
| Special needs | 8% | 24% | 32% | 36% |
| Child trafficking | 5% | 21% | 32% | 42% |
| Clean water | 6% | 17% | 29% | 48% |
| Refugee response | 5% | 17% | 24% | 54% |
| Gender equality | 4% | 14% | 23% | 59% |
| Medical aid | 2% | 10% | 22% | 66% |
| Political activism | 2% | 11% | 17% | 69% |
| Environmental issues | 1% | 9% | 18% | 72% |
| Global warming | 1% | 6% | 12% | 81% |

May 2017, n=609 pastors.

poverty (1%). Even so, it's notable that a majority of pastors (56%) tends to think their churches should be more involved with helping the global poor. Younger pastors (68% of those under age 40) are the most likely to express this sentiment, which could be associated with the justice inclinations of their generation or the ambitious energy of being in the first part of one's ministry tenure.

Pastors generally appear to feel less satisfied with—or perhaps, as leaders, just more analytical of—their church's current anti-poverty efforts when compared to practicing Christians, a minority of whom (43%) feels their church should be more involved. Practicing Christians are more likely than pastors to say that their church has an "above average" sense of urgency about global poverty (30% vs. 21% of pastors), while pastors are more willing to deem it "below average" (21% vs. 5% of practicing Christians). There is an upward trend, however, among practicing Christians who say their church could do more in this respect, with a 6-percentage-point increase between 2011 and 2013, and another 7-percentage-point increase between 2013 and 2017.

Though pastors' generally unfavorable assessments of their churches' activity against poverty may feel discouraging (particularly in contrast to individual Christians' more optimistic reviews), there's more to this story—and it's somewhat positive.

First of all, nobody would deny there *is* more work to be done to end poverty, and it seems pastors want the Church in the U.S. to be an increasingly productive if not leading member of that work.

Additionally, Barna finds that a pastor's sense of his or her church's involvement is likely formed in proportion to awareness of the issue of global poverty, rather than the church's actual involvement. In other words, the church leaders who are most concerned about and / or doing the most to address poverty are often the same ones who hope their ministry might achieve more—a continuation of the idea that the more you care, the more you care (see infographic on page 54). Meanwhile, the pastors who appear less mindful of or familiar with global poverty work are those more likely to already feel content with their church's level of involvement. This indicates yet again how an awareness of Christian compassion and responsibility for the world's poor is rarely static or satiated, no matter the level of involvement or the advances made.

Pastors generally appear to feel less satisfied with their church's current anti-poverty efforts when compared to practicing Christians

## Should Your Church Be More or Less Involved in Helping the Global Poor?

■ More
■ Same
■ Less

Pastors
56%
44%
1%

Practicing Christians
43%
54%
4%

May 2017, *n*=219 practicing Christians, 609 pastors.

## How Much Urgency Does Your Church Feel for Helping the World's Poor?

■ Above-average sense of urgency
■ Average sense of urgency
■ Below-average sense of urgency

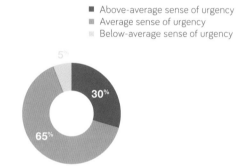

Pastors — 21%, 21%, 58%

Practicing Christians — 5%, 30%, 65%

May 2017, *n*= 219 practicing Christians, 609 pastors.

## A POVERTY LESSON PLAN

It's vital that church leaders not only experience a Christian compassion for the poor, wherever they live, but also have the tools to make informed, effective contributions in the fight against poverty. While just more than a third of pastors (36%) is "pretty" or "extremely" interested in learning more about topics that have to do with global poverty, their actions show that they are accumulating knowledge about poverty in many ways.

## Pastors' Interest in Learning About Aspects of Poverty

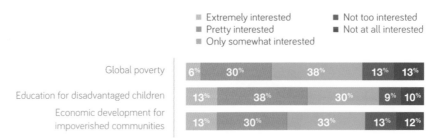

■ Extremely interested   ■ Not too interested
■ Pretty interested      ■ Not at all interested
■ Only somewhat interested

| | | | | | |
|---|---|---|---|---|---|
| Global poverty | 6% | 30% | 38% | 13% | 13% |
| Education for disadvantaged children | 13% | 38% | 30% | 9% | 10% |
| Economic development for impoverished communities | 13% | 30% | 33% | 13% | 12% |

May 2017, *n*=609 pastors.

A majority of pastors (62%) has read a magazine article about poverty in the past three months. Significant minorities of pastors have also learned about poverty through online videos (39%), documentaries (39%), talks or lectures (34%) and books (23%) during that time.

Given the different ways that generations interact with various media and devices, a pastor's age influences the ways he or she might receive information about poverty. Pastors who are older than 50 are highly likely to read magazine articles (69%), for example, while pastors under 40 gravitate toward online videos (51%).

There are most likely varying levels of intention and attention here—for example, the question specifies that the individual has merely watched "at least 15 minutes" of a documentary. There may be some overlap in the categories of online videos, documentaries and talks, and it's unclear how many pastors are actively and consistently seeking out these poverty messages versus how many are stumbling upon them.

Regardless, a promising cycle of gaining and sharing information emerges among senior pastors: Pastors who report preaching about poverty at least three times in the past year have also spent that time gleaning insight about poverty from magazine articles (81%), videos (64%), documentaries (60%), talks (59%) and books (44%). They are often at least pretty interested in learning more about education (72%), economic development (57%) and global poverty in general (56%). On the other hand, pastors who do not speak on poverty are less likely to show enthusiasm about exploring these topics (35%, 29% and 20%, respectively).

A promising cycle of gaining and sharing information emerges among senior pastors

## How Pastors Are Learning About Poverty, by Age

*(activities in the last three months)*

- 51 and older
- 40–50
- Under 40
- All pastors

Read a magazine article about poverty
**69%**
**53%**
55%
62%

Watched an online video about global poverty
**38%**
**30%**
51%
39%

Watched at least 15 minutes of a documentary about poverty
**43%**
**32%**
35%
39%

Listened to a talk at a conference or event about poverty
**37%**
**27%**
35%
34%

Read a book about poverty
**23%**
**22%**
25%
23%

May 2017, n=609 pastors.

Personal instruction and personal concern are also correlated. Of pastors who feel an extreme burden for global poverty, majorities have read an article (78%) or viewed a documentary film (55%) or video (51%) that touched on it. More than a third (36%) report learning about poverty in a book. The differences on these responses are stark, anywhere from 11- to 25-percentage-points higher than the average pastor.

When pastors do intentionally seek out information about poverty, they are usually thinking practically. More than two-thirds (68%) hope their search yields ideas to implement, while 41 percent would like a tangible resource they can put to use. Over half (56%) look for a biblical perspective or stories of how Christians and churches respond to social justice. A similar percentage (55%) looks for facts and statistics that might help their understanding of poverty.

This hunt for spiritual and tangible solutions is yet another statistical example of the great intensity with which American pastors approach international poverty—a seriousness that, when strengthened by reliable information, generous church members and smart partnerships, can be a guiding force in lifting people out of poverty.

## Pastors Most Want Ideas to Implement

When trying to understand poverty issues, what kind of information are you looking for?

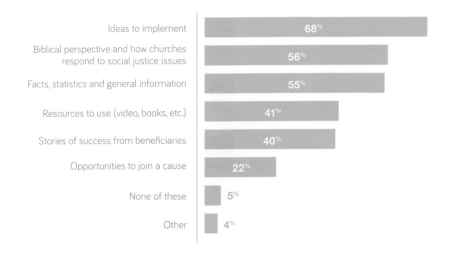

| | |
|---|---|
| Ideas to implement | 68% |
| Biblical perspective and how churches respond to social justice issues | 56% |
| Facts, statistics and general information | 55% |
| Resources to use (video, books, etc.) | 41% |
| Stories of success from beneficiaries | 40% |
| Opportunities to join a cause | 22% |
| None of these | 5% |
| Other | 4% |

May 2017, n=609 pastors.

# THE GLOBAL REACH OF THE PULPIT

## How church leaders are using their influence to confront poverty

A strong majority of the American public (88%), including 92 percent of practicing Christians, trusts the opinion of a pastor when it comes to the issue of global poverty. How often, and in which contexts, are church leaders communicating their ideas about caring for the poor?

A slight majority has taught or preached about international poverty in church**

More than half have talked about poverty with children in their family or close circle*

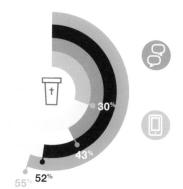

**30%**

**43%**

55% **52%**

43 percent have tried to persuade someone else to volunteer or donate for the poor*

Three in 10 pastors have posted about poverty on personal social media*

---

When pastors and their churches have a higher sense of involvement in ending poverty, leaders are more likely to report participating in influential activities, like encouraging compassion in younger generations

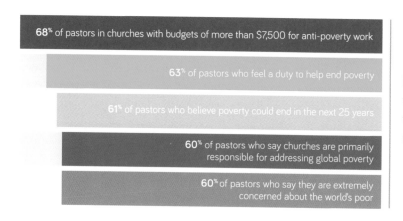

**68%** of pastors in churches with budgets of more than $7,500 for anti-poverty work

**63%** of pastors who feel a duty to help end poverty

**61%** of pastors who believe poverty could end in the next 25 years

**60%** of pastors who say churches are primarily responsible for addressing global poverty

**60%** of pastors who say they are extremely concerned about the world's poor

have spoken to children they know about the topic of global poverty in recent months

*in the past three months **in the past year
May 2017, *n*=609 pastors.

# HOW OUR CHURCH TAKES ACTION ON POVERTY

Q What is the importance of addressing global poverty as a church?

**JESSY PADILLA**

Pastor of Iglesia Emanuel
in Waukegan, Illinois

To set the context of the importance of addressing global poverty as a church, first I want to address the mission of the Church at large. In Matthew 28:18-20, Jesus commissions us to make disciples in all nations. At Iglesia Emanuel, we embrace that commission. Only people who clearly understand and practice discipleship understand this call. To be a disciple means to invest your life into the life of another and to be Christ incarnate for others. I've been leading mission trips for 30 years. Most of the time it is in the context of poverty. It's hard to bring the gospel to the poor if you don't bring something that is tangible. We show the visible love of God by addressing their poverty first, so that they are open to understand that he is interested in having a relationship with them.

We want our people to understand that their purpose in life doesn't come from a title, a job, money or opportunity. Purpose comes from the gospel—knowing it and sharing it. As a church, we do this together.

Q Tell us about one way you've chosen to address global poverty as a church.

One Sunday, Compassion International brought an exhibition to show people what it is like to live in extreme poverty and to see the child sponsorship program in action. Child sponsorship provides food, medicine and other stuff that really helps the child understand they are important. But that's not the end: Each child needs to understand the gospel and the depth of God's love. Where else will they get this teaching if not through the Church? We chose to be globally engaged with an organization that is doing the same thing we are doing as a church: sharing the gospel and making disciples of Jesus Christ.

For our people, the monthly financial sacrifice is small, and our people understand it's a totally different investment than giving to the church. It's an intentional way to bless the poor, to show God's love, to share the gospel and to make disciples. Child sponsorship is as spiritually benefitting to the sponsor as it is to the child in poverty.

Q What are some effective ways to rally and involve congregants for the long term?

By writing letters to the children, the sponsors in our church have the ability to share the gospel, to encourage a child in the faith and to remind a child of God's love and faithfulness regardless of the circumstance. By praying for their sponsored children, sponsors in our church are modeling Christ's compassion to their own children. Writing and praying allow parents in our church to pass on biblical faith values to the next generation.

Our congregation has a lot of first-generation adults, so it is easy for them to identify with children in developing countries who live in poverty. For example, there is a 25-year-old young man from Mexico. Both of his parents died when he was young. He was all alone and really needed an advocate. As an adult when he was given the opportunity to sponsor a child in Honduras, he said yes right away. As a sponsor, he knew that the child would have an advocate whenever he needed one. And that really resonates with his background. I'm also reminded of an older woman in our church who has no family members in the United States. Outside of our church community, she is really alone. She works a few hours a week in order to provide for her simple needs.

But she responded right away to child sponsorship because she identifies with the child's situation. The letter exchange is very meaningful to this sponsor because the child appreciates her and prays for her, and that is a big source of joy for this sponsor. The sponsor trusts God to provide her basic necessities, and in faith believes God will help her provide for this child. It's like the widow's mite—giving a small amount, yet it is a big percentage of all that she has.

# INSPIRING INVOLVEMENT

4

## A LOOK AT THE CATALYSTS FOR—AND THE BARRIERS TO—POVERTY ENGAGEMENT

The data in this report has shown how Americans with a vibrant commitment to Christianity and an active church life are often front-and-center in anti-poverty work. They are propelled by a conviction that they can, and should, make a difference—and they often do.

Considering the vast evidence of the hard work of governments, non-profits, ministries and individuals addressing material poverty around the world, many experts reason that the pattern of progress will continue, culminating in the eventual end of global poverty, perhaps even within our lifetime.[54] The American Church, which includes a segment of eager volunteers and donors and is driven by a scriptural directive to care for the poor, then emerges as a natural leader in this mission.

What's stopping us?

## PERCEIVED BARRIERS

As earlier chapters detailed, practicing Christians' sense of personal responsibility for poverty is increasing, as well as their optimism that ending extreme poverty may be a realistic goal. Correspondingly, practicing Christians in 2017 are slow to name reasons or excuses that may make people hesitant to get involved concerning poverty.

Among the top barriers identified, however, a theme emerges—one of caution or cynicism. Roughly one-third struggles to trust governments in countries that need aid (35%), choose a non-profit that inspires confidence (35%), find a place to start (33%), spend resources on foreign concerns rather than U.S. problems (32%) or simply to believe that what they do could make a meaningful difference (32%).

Given the high chance that pastors encounter—or potentially misunderstand—a variety of motivations and experiences in the communities they

### Reasons People Are Reluctant to Help End Global Poverty

■ Pastors
■ Practicing Christians

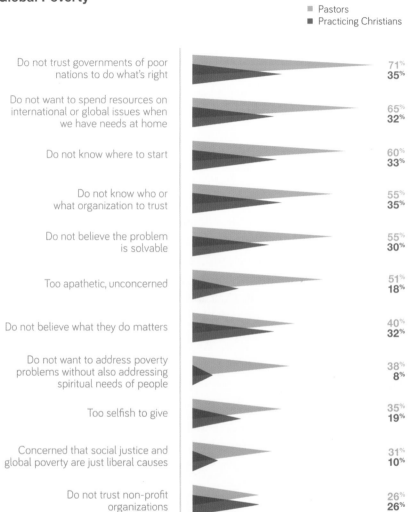

| Reason | Pastors | Practicing Christians |
|---|---|---|
| Do not trust governments of poor nations to do what's right | 71% | 35% |
| Do not want to spend resources on international or global issues when we have needs at home | 65% | 32% |
| Do not know where to start | 60% | 33% |
| Do not know who or what organization to trust | 55% | 35% |
| Do not believe the problem is solvable | 55% | 30% |
| Too apathetic, unconcerned | 51% | 18% |
| Do not believe what they do matters | 40% | 32% |
| Do not want to address poverty problems without also addressing spiritual needs of people | 38% | 8% |
| Too selfish to give | 35% | 19% |
| Concerned that social justice and global poverty are just liberal causes | 31% | 10% |
| Do not trust non-profit organizations | 26% | 26% |

May 2017, *n*=609 pastors, 219 practicing Christians.

lead, they are more likely than practicing Christians to select almost *any* reason for the absence of action on poverty. Pastors primarily point to a lack of trust in the governments of poor countries (71%) or to the idea that domestic problems should be solved first before focusing internationally (65%). Many ministers propose (or project) that it all may be a little too overwhelming: A majority thinks people do not know where to start (60%), do not know which organizations to trust (55%), do not believe global poverty is solvable (55%) or are apathetic about the issue (51%). More than one in three pastors (35%) goes so far as to pin inactivity regarding poverty on selfishness. A quarter of pastors (26%) agrees (with an equal proportion of practicing Christians) that people are hesitant to trust non-profits.

This report has repeatedly recorded some of respondents' wariness about, or at least confusion regarding, the Church's intersection with what may be seen as political ground. The tension surfaces again here, with nearly a third of pastors (31%) assuming that individuals refrain from action on poverty because it may be lumped in with "liberal causes."

Pastors in churches that do not donate to anti-poverty efforts are more likely to assume their congregants don't act because they're hoping to address spiritual needs first and foremost (57% vs. 34% of pastors in churches that do donate for poverty). It's possible, though, that these pastors could be reflecting their own reasons for refraining from financial investment in working against poverty.

## PATTERNS IN PREVIOUS ENGAGEMENT

The main reasons people say they have gotten involved in a cause in the past are primarily emotional: They believed they could make a difference (62%) or they saw or heard a moving story (45%). More than a third of adults remembers being driven by an overwhelming sense of purpose (38%) or a relationship with someone who was already involved in the cause (34%). Direct requests for involvement seem to be

## PUT IT TO USE

### Think

Millennials are often dismissed as the "slacktivist" generation, but Barna's extensive study of this group shows that they crave relationships and a sense of purpose. This is key to their discipleship and involvement in churches. On the issue of poverty, they are ready to be put to work, to be connected with other supporters and to be of use online *and* in person.

### Ask

How does your church allow *all* generations—young and old—to work together in addressing poverty, celebrating their unique strengths without belittling one or the other?

## "I First Got Involved with a Cause Because ..."

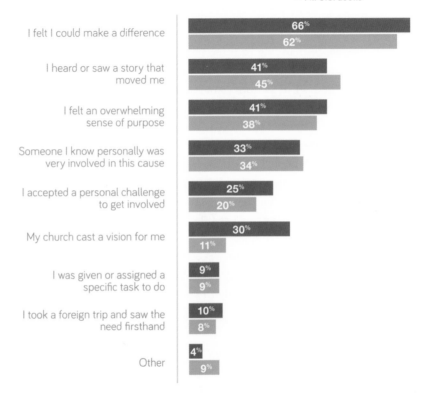

■ Practicing Christians
■ All U.S. adults

| | Practicing Christians | All U.S. adults |
|---|---|---|
| I felt I could make a difference | 66% | 62% |
| I heard or saw a story that moved me | 41% | 45% |
| I felt an overwhelming sense of purpose | 41% | 38% |
| Someone I know personally was very involved in this cause | 33% | 34% |
| I accepted a personal challenge to get involved | 25% | 20% |
| My church cast a vision for me | 30% | 11% |
| I was given or assigned a specific task to do | 9% | 9% |
| I took a foreign trip and saw the need firsthand | 10% | 8% |
| Other | 4% | 9% |

May 2017, *n*=1,001 U.S. adults, *n*=219 practicing Christians.

## Reasons for Choosing an Organization to Support

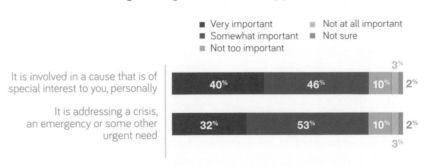

■ Very important   ■ Not at all important
■ Somewhat important   ■ Not sure
■ Not too important

| | Very important | Somewhat important | Not too important | Not at all important | Not sure |
|---|---|---|---|---|---|
| It is involved in a cause that is of special interest to you, personally | 40% | 46% | 10% | 3% | 2% |
| It is addressing a crisis, an emergency or some other urgent need | 32% | 53% | 10% | 3% | 2% |

May 2017, *n*=1,001 U.S. adults.

less convincing—few say that they joined a cause because they were explicitly challenged (20%) or asked (9%) to. However, such pleas may be more effective within the context of church attendance and faith commitment. Three in 10 practicing Christians (30%) took up a cause because their church "cast a vision" for it.

The motivations for selecting a specific organization to support are also often made on an emotional, heart-centered level. A special, personal interest is the most important factor (40% "very" + 46% "somewhat"), followed by a desire to address an immediate need or emergency (32% "very" + 53% "somewhat"). People are less likely to be aware of (or admit to) making these decisions based on factors like social pressure or convenience, though certainly even their understanding of personal values or urgent crises are formed in these contexts.

## HOPE FOR THE WORLD

Many factors might influence whether people decide to help someone else, including the urgency, approachability, morality or probability of an issue. But feelings are unavoidable in the formula of poverty engagement. Activists, fundraisers, marketers and ministers may wonder, what are the most galvanizing emotions?

**If You Knew Ending Global Poverty Was Possible, Would You Do More?**

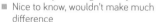

■ More likely to do significantly more
■ Nice to know, wouldn't make much difference

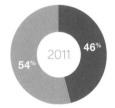
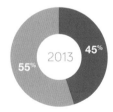

2011, *n*=995 U.S. adults; 2013, *n*=1,014 U.S. adults; May 2017, *n*=1,001 U.S. adults.

## PUT IT TO USE

 **Think**

Forty-five percent of U.S. adults would donate more for global poverty if they knew the specific impact of their donation. Organizations and ministries working toward poverty reduction should set the tone in celebrating successes.

 **Do**

As your church develops a long-term, holistic strategy in caring for the world's poor, make "progress reports" part of that routine. Transparency about donations and their impact boosts trust and optimism—both of which are connected to increased engagement.

Among the respondents in this survey, hope—both in poverty's potential end and one's ability to take part in that—is connected to robust concern for and work against poverty. It'd be naïve to assume optimism is universally helpful; for example, other research shows that optimistic people are more likely to back out when circumstances are unfavorable, just as they are more likely to take action when circumstances are favorable.[55] People who are happy are also more likely than people who are sad to apply stereotypes to individuals.[56] However, a good mood also makes people more helpful toward others[57]—and sometimes kicks off a cycle of feeling good about being helpful, and being helpful because it feels good.[58]

Quite simply, Barna observes that people who are hopeful that they can make a difference are those more willing to *try*. A majority of U.S. adults (57%)—11 percentage points more than in 2011—says that knowing it is possible to end extreme global poverty would make them do significantly more to help bring that about. Among practicing Christians, the percentage climbs to 62 percent.

It's possible that the internet could be a contributing factor here. Social media gives Americans a front-row seat, so to speak, to global concerns, natural disasters and systemic injustices. Being online also fosters solidarity and connection in the midst of them. This has become increasingly true in the years since the last time these questions were posed to respondents. It's difficult for more fortunate or privileged individuals today to claim ignorance of global problems—or of their responsibility or potential to affect them. While there may be good reasons to bemoan the distraction and cynicism that our digital world may bring, it does engender a sense of accountability.

Technological advancements also make it easier to have access to information about the specific effect of monetary gifts. For most people, any evidence of one's financial impact would encourage them to give more. This is very true of Millennials (62%, compared to 32% of older generations), an age group that places a high value on information and transparency. This "show your work" approach could be particularly helpful in retaining a majority of non-white Americans (57%) as donors (compared to 38% of white Americans).

Overall, most U.S. adults and Christians, if they have some assurance that they could have an impact, would be willing to play their part in combating poverty and its ills—another testament to the animating effect of optimism and confidence.

# A HOLISTIC VIEW
# OF POVERTY

## Q&A WITH MARK BOWERS

Throughout his tenure at the Chalmers Center, Mark has overseen the research, development and pilot-test of their U.S. and international development curriculum. He also developed training of trainers (TOT) processes to equip facilitators and partners to use non-formal microfinance, financial education and jobs readiness tools in their communities. Mark earned a BA in Psychology and an MA in Intercultural Studies while teaching at Quy Nhon University of Pedagogy in Vietnam. Outside of work, Mark loves creating travel adventures with his wife, Tannia, and their new baby boy, Elias.

**J. MARK BOWERS**
Director of design & engagement
at the Chalmers Center

Q A majority of U.S. adults incorrectly assumes international poverty has increased in the past 25 years, even though millions have been lifted out of poverty in that time. If progress has occurred / is occurring even while most Americans seem to be a bit out of touch on this issue, why is it still significant to be educating donors and the Church on the realities and best practices of poverty alleviation?

Even with this news that global economic mobility is on the rise, the Church still has a calling that has yet to be fulfilled: to proclaim and put to practice the good news of the Kingdom reign of God, over *all* of creation and among the poor. We have to be careful as a Church that we don't fully equate social and economic mobility with poverty alleviation. While God's blessing does have a material component, that is just *one* sign of his favor.

Jesus was always talking about finances—and not just as some material matter, but as a spiritual matter. That's a big contrast to this dualistic thinking of today that divorces the sacred and the secular. In proper context, the countless teachings and parables of Jesus about wealth, possessions and the Kingdom of God simply don't make sense as messages of individual fulfillment, try as some may. When we examine Old Testament economic customs like Jubilee, Gleaning, Sabbath, we'll find laws that God set up to assure that there would be justice and peace. Since the beginning, money has always held a central place in God's work, and the local church has a unique role to play in demonstrating the kind of financial *shalom* that we're supposed to aim for and bring about in the world. That biblical *shalom* is not the same thing as secular social mobility.

The Church is there to call people of all income levels to ultimately see that God is the one who is providing for us and not ourselves. It's reminding us again that, while financial flourishing might be one sign of God's blessing, it's not the end goal. According to a holistic definition of poverty, we are all poor, materially or not, and strive to be transformed day-by-day into God's glorious image.

> "Biblical *shalom* is not the same thing as secular social mobility."

Q Why do pastors have a unique role to play in helping the poor, even in a time marked by secularization and less trust of faith leaders on other major topics?

When you are trying to practice the economy of Jesus among people who are poor—with your neighbors, your friends or community members—I can't think of a better person than a pastor who can help to guide you. That's their role in the church, to shepherd and to guide us through what living out the Kingdom of God looks like. A pastor is really the ultimate steward of the people of God—and having a place where they can work out these kind of complicated economic issues in a community of trust is vital for growth.

Q What are common mistakes or misconceptions that might keep people from really being able to play their unique role?

In the history of the church, we've done terrible things to people who are poor and marginalized in the name of God. God help us to never do those things again. But at the same time, let's not let that fear of repeating harm paralyze us. Let's walk forward in faith and humility as learners in these relationships. Instead of saying, *Don't, you're just going to hurt people*, we're trying to say, *What are the best practices? How can you actually help in ways that are mutually healthy?* Don't let that fear of hurting stunt you. Don't just cancel your ministries; remake them. Reimagine them. The Chalmers Center has created courses like "Are You a Good Neighbor?" to help church members ask themselves and their leaders questions like: How do we practice hospitality toward the poor? Even more importantly, do we know how to receive from people who are poor? What do we communicate in the physical spaces where we live, work and shop? In our churches, how do our spending habits, the style of worship, the language options and the level of literacy make the Kingdom accessible to others?

> "Let's walk forward in faith and humility as learners in these relationships."

 How can the U.S. Church ensure that the voices of the marginalized help shape efforts to help the poor?

I'm a white male. I'm in my 30s. I have inherited a legacy, especially in my nation, of economic systems that have actually helped me to succeed. It's easy to say, "Well, I worked hard for my success," and not recognize the collective history that's helped me to do that. That individualistic perspective doesn't see when systems, in the U.S. or around the world, work well for me—but might not work well for everyone else.

Part of recognizing privilege means that we intentionally place ourselves under the leadership of Christians who are marginalized so that they can shape our walk with God and the way we do economic development ministry. On a personal level, consider your mentors: Are any of them of a different race or lower socioeconomic position than you are? On a church or local community level, are those with privilege willing to cede power to someone of a minority ethnicity, lower educational level or lower economic status? Those questions serve as a litmus test for how ready we truly are to include the voices of our brothers and sisters on the margins.

# PAYING IT FORWARD

## Q&A WITH EMI HERNANDEZ

Since graduating from Compassion International's Leadership Development Program about 18 years ago, Emi has gotten her degree in accounting and started her family. Currently, she splits her time between training Japanese professionals in business English, bookkeeping for a non-profit organization and running a ministry for children in a local slum community, which she founded with her husband in 2014.

**EMI HERNANDEZ**
Compassion sponsorship alumna, accountant, minister

Q The data shows that people who are personally touched by poverty (by living in or near it) are often the ones who have the highest levels of concern about poverty and show a tendency to get involved to help other people in turn. Does this confirm your own experience?

As someone who has experienced firsthand what it was like to lack in resources such as food, clothing, school supplies and finances, and having come out of that situation by the help of the ministry of Compassion International, I have this deep sense of gratitude for how my life was changed. This compels me to be of help to others facing the same situation that I came out of in any way I can. I would say that it's a combination of wanting to pay it forward and also the firm conviction that the acts of help that we do *indeed* make a difference. Opportunities to help can be in different forms: Not only did I gain from the financial assistance that I received for my schooling, but I also experienced mentorship, discipleship, fellowship and that sense of having value as a person because God loves me. Because the impact of those experiences changed me, I want to be able to somehow provide the same to others in my own capacity. Because I know what it was like to be in that place of need, I am able to empathize. Because I was helped and the help made a difference in my life, I know for a fact that the help I give will do the same to others.

 When it comes to getting people involved in helping those in need, encouragement and empowerment can be motivating emotions. Why do you think this is?

When we respond because of anger or sadness, there's bound to be an object of that negative emotion—it could be the government, "the system," the people themselves facing that situation. We could give grudgingly with the thought that it is somebody else's responsibility to address these people's needs. I believe that when we are encouraged or challenged to help, it creates a more positive impact on us and makes us realize that there is something that we can do to change the situation. We take responsibility as people who are part of the bigger community outside of our own neighborhood; we become actors and not spectators. The concerted effort of individuals may not resolve the issue for all of the world, but it will make a difference for some people at least.

 As someone who was sponsored as a child, do you think early intervention is important?

Without a doubt, lack of education is one of the underlying causes of poverty. In context, a child who is poor may not go to school for any of the following reasons: he is hungry because there's no food to eat at home; he doesn't have fare money to go to school; he's unable to comply with the school projects because of no money; he is forced to find ways to support himself and his family either by begging or finding odd jobs. When he misses school, he misses the opportunity to be equipped with the knowledge and skills that would give him a fair chance in life.

In reality, when a child has missed a year or more in school, it is easier for that child to give up on the idea of finishing school because he is behind for his age and he tends to be embarrassed about it. When early intervention in education is given while the child is still young, combined with other programs that address the other needs of the child, it minimizes the likelihood of the child continuing that cycle of poverty into adulthood, thereby changing the course of his life.

In the Philippines, where I come from, people who have not finished college have few opportunities to find better jobs that give them decent pay and allow them to support themselves and their families. In our work with children in poverty, we know kids who have dropped out of school because they feel they're getting too old for their grade level, or they are unable to attend school regularly because of financial issues. In most cases, the parent or guardian of the children did not pursue their own schooling in their time for the same reasons. Education—starting at a young age and with continuity—can break this cycle and is sure to make a difference.

In my case, I was already in 5th grade when I got accepted in the Family Helper Program of Compassion in 1991. Back then, it did not have much of an impact to me. However, because I was part of the program, and I met other specific requirements, it qualified me to apply for the Leadership Development Program when it was pioneered in the Philippines in 1996. This program greatly impacted my life, as it gave me the opportunity to go to college and get a degree and then find a great job. It definitely changed my life.

Q Beyond bringing people to a place of financial stability, what do you believe should be the end goals and outcomes of poverty alleviation work?

Addressing poverty is not just about meeting the physical needs of the person. Beyond the economic issues, people in poverty situations face underlying issues of self-worth and hopelessness that are magnified by their struggles in their everyday life. Yes, providing financial and material assistance helps, but the need to address the spiritual needs of these people should not be overlooked. When we find Christ, we find hope and the courage to believe that life can be different for us going forward. The goal of spiritual transformation has to go hand-in-hand with poverty alleviation for greater impact.

"The goal of spiritual transformation has to go hand-in-hand with poverty alleviation for greater impact."

# CONCLUSION

## INCREASING YOUR CHURCH'S IMPACT
## IN THE GLOBAL POVERTY FIGHT
By Roxanne Stone, editor in chief for Barna Group

*Knowledge is power.* You've heard this, of course, and at Barna our hope is that we've empowered you with the knowledge you've read in this report. Through the data, infographics, interviews and research, we aspire to inform you in your work to combat global poverty.

But, as we've seen over and over in this report, knowledge can only go so far. Many well-informed, well-educated people still remain cynical or cautious when it comes to fighting global poverty. At the same time, many people who feel concern or even personal responsibility for addressing poverty exhibit a lack of awareness about the subject. Which prompts the question: *What do you do with this knowledge from this study?* If there is one thing that makes us sad as researchers at Barna, it's when our work is read once, shelved and forgotten about. Knowledge must be turned into action.

As a spiritual leader, how can you use this research to guide your efforts to serve the poor? How can you use what you've learned here to inspire greater engagement in the people you lead?

There are a few key takeaways from this research that I think can help.

## People are looking to you!

The world wants pastors and their churches to take the lead in fighting global poverty. Christians, especially, see pastors as influential and well-positioned to address poverty. They are seeking leadership in understanding and action from the Church. This study reveals that pastors do have authority to speak about topics of poverty with those in their pews. Additionally, there is an opportunity with many who might be outside the Church—the research reveals that younger Americans and liberals, in particular, want to see the Church do *more* to address global poverty.

### Make it personal.

The more people are able to feel personally connected to the work you are doing, the more apt they are to stay engaged. Tell stories of the people you are working with; share how your efforts are making a difference; let people from your congregation share their own experiences in serving the poor. Consider choosing one cause and / or ministry a month to highlight, with a few words on this partnership or project every week from the pulpit.

Celebrate success. Hope is a powerful motivator in the poverty fight. Optimism about ending poverty and about one's role in that effort are connected to engagement. When people believe what they are doing is actually making a difference, they are encouraged and maintain interest. Make time to cheer for the good work your church is doing and for the tangible effects you are having.

### Publicize your efforts.

One barrier people identify as keeping them from serving the poor is a simple lack of information. They don't know what to do or where to start. Don't shy away from making the opportunities to serve known to people—put it on your website, talk about it during announcements, have booths or sign-up sheets available in your foyer and enlist small group leaders to register their groups.

Look to the margins. Minorities and a small group of highly engaged volunteers are some of the most optimistic, interested and active in poverty reduction. Come alongside those in your church who are already working in these areas and ask them how the church can help. Look to them as leaders and advocates in your ministries that serve the poor.

### Don't be afraid of scarcity or confused priorities.

The research in this report reveals time and again that the more you care, the more you care. Meaning, people who deeply care about and are engaged with domestic poverty are also the ones who express concern about global poverty. Those who donate to missions are more likely to also donate to global poverty. People have room in their hearts (and often in their wallets!) to care about more than one or two issues.

## Take heart!

Practicing Christians are the most engaged segment of the population when it comes to fighting poverty. Local churches are already doing many things right in discipling Christians toward compassion for the poor. But there is more to do: Fighting poverty—both material and spiritual—will *always* be the mission of the Church. We pray this report—both the data and the stories—will be an encouragement and a spark as you press into this mission.

# NOTES

1. "Nearly 385 million children living in extreme poverty, says joint World Bank Group – UNICEF study," UNICEF, https://www.unicef.org/media/media_92856.html (accessed March 7, 2018).

2. The extreme poverty line was set in 1990, then adjusted for inflation. It's determined by the International Comparison Program (http://www.worldbank.org/en/topic/poverty/brief/global-poverty-line-faq).

3. "Poverty Overview," The World Bank, http://www.worldbank.org/en/topic/poverty/overview (accessed January 19, 2018).

4. "Poverty Overview," The World Bank.

5. "World Bank Forecasts Global Poverty to Fall Below 10% for First Time; Major Hurdles Remain in Goal to End Poverty by 2030," The World Bank, http://www.worldbank.org/en/news/press-release/2015/10/04/world-bank-forecasts-global-poverty-to-fall-below-10-for-first-time-major-hurdles-remain-in-goal-to-end-poverty-by-2030 (accessed January 19, 2018).

6. "The World Factbook," Central Intelligence Agency, https://www.cia.gov/library/publications/the-world-factbook/fields/2046.html (accessed January 19, 2018).

7. "Does polio still exist?" World Health Organization, http://www.who.int/features/qa/07/en/ (accessed January 19, 2018).

8. Katherine Kornei, "Here are some of the world's worst cities for air quality," *Science Magazine,* May 21, 2017, http://www.sciencemag.org/news/2017/03/here-are-some-world-s-worst-cities-air-quality (accessed January 19, 2018).

9. "Corruption Perceptions Index 2016," Transparency International, January 25, 2017, https://www.transparency.org/news/feature/corruption_perceptions_index_2016#table (accessed January 19, 2018).

10. "Poverty Reduction Begins with Children," UNICEF, March 2000, http://www.albacharia.ma/xmlui/bitstream/handle/123456789/30755/0512Poverty%20Reduction%20Begins%20with%20Children%20(2000).pdf?sequence=1 (accessed January 19, 2018).

11. Dave Umhoefer, "U.S. Rep. Ron Kind says that 'thanks to Medicare,' 75% fewer seniors are in poverty, and most have health coverage," Politifact, August 25, 2011, http://www.politifact.com/wisconsin/statements/2011/aug/25/ron-kind/us-rep-ron-kind-says-thanks-medicare-75-fewer-seni/ (accessed January 19, 2018).

12. "Norman Borlaug – Biographical," Nobelprize.org, https://www.nobelprize.org/nobel_prizes/peace/laureates/1970/borlaug-bio.html (accessed January 19, 2018).

13. James Feyrer, Dimitra Politi and David N. Weil, "The Cognitive Effects of Micronutrient Deficiency: Evidence from Salt Iodization in the United States," *Journal of the European Economic Association* Volume 15.2, July 2013, p. 355–387.

14. "Business and International Development: Opportunities, Responsibilities and Expectations," Edelman, January 2005, https://sites.hks.harvard.edu/m-rcbg/CSRI/publications/report_5_edelman_survey.pdf (accessed January 19, 2018).

15. "Famine menaces 20m people in Africa and Yemen," *The Economist,* May 30, 2017, https://www.economist.com/news/middle-east-and-africa/21719827-war-not-drought-reason-people-are-starving-famine-menaces-20m-people (accessed January 19, 2018).

16. "Unlocking the Water Potential of Africa," Food and Agriculture Organization of the United Nations, 2003, http://www.fao.org/docrep/006/y4525e/y4525e04.htm (accessed January 19, 2018.)

17. "Poverty and Development," Transparency International, https://www.transparency.org/topic/detail/poverty_and_development (accessed January 19, 2018).

18. "IMF Survey: IMF Study Explores How to Better Manage Government Pay and Employment," International Monetary Fund, June 9, 2016, https://www.imf.org/en/News/Articles/2015/09/28/04/53/sores060916a (accessed January 19, 2018).

19. Bianca DiJulio, "Data Note: Americans' Views On The U.S. Role In Global Health," The Henry J. Kaiser Family Foundation, January 23, 2015, https://www.kff.org/global-health-policy/poll-finding/data-note-americans-views-on-the-u-s-role-in-global-health/ (accessed January 19, 2018).

20. "The Issue," 1,000 Days, http://thousanddays.org/the-issue/ (accessed January 19, 2018).

21. "Under-Five Mortality," UNICEF, https://data.unicef.org/topic/child-survival/under-five-mortality/ (accessed January 19, 2018).

22. "The State of Food Security and Nutrition in the World 2017," Food and Agriculture Organization of the United Nations, http://www.fao.org/state-of-food-security-nutrition/en/ (accessed January 19, 2018).

23. "Investing in All God's Children," Faith for International Assistance, http://www.faithforinternationalassistance.org/investing-in-all-gods-children.html (accessed January 19, 2018).

24. Additional sources recommended by Dr. Brewster include *The Child in South Asia* by David P. Haxton (UNICEF, 1988) and "World Declaration on the Survival, Protection and Development of Children" (UNICEF, 1990.)

25. *The Generosity Gap* (Ventura, CA: Barna Group, 2017).

26. If 116,926,305 U.S. households (as estimated by the United States Census Bureau: https://factfinder.census.gov/faces/tableservices/jsf/pages/productview.xhtml?src=bkmk) gave the average reported donation from Barna's study ($434), total U.S. donations would be $50,746,016,370. In other words, child poverty donations ought to be a $51 billion industry if people are reporting correctly and the survey is representative. This might be a reasonable estimation, considering the many causes covered by that category, as indicated here: https://www.charitynavigator.org/index.cfm?bay=content.view&cpid=42.

27. "Americans Soften on Immigration in 2017," Barna Group, September 19, 2017,

https://www.barna.com/research/americans-soften-immigration-2017/ (accessed March 7, 2018).

28. "Volunteering in the United States, 2015," Bureau of Labor Statistics, https://www.bls.gov/news.release/volun.nr0.htm (accessed January 19, 2018).

29. "Volunteering in the United States, 2015," Bureau of Labor Statistics.

30. *The Generosity Gap.*

31. *The Generosity Gap.*

32. "Wealth, Asset Ownership, & Debt of Households Detailed Tables: 2013," United States Census Bureau, https://www.census.gov/data/tables/2013/demo/wealth/wealth-asset-ownership.html (accessed January 19, 2018).

33. Catherine Rampell, "Marriage Is for Rich People," *The New York Times,* February 6, 2012, https://economix.blogs.nytimes.com/2012/02/06/marriage-is-for-rich-people/ (accessed January 19, 2018).

34. "Wealth, Asset Ownership, & Debt of Households Detailed Tables: 2013," United States Census Bureau.

35. Pam Fessler, "Study Reveals the Geography of Charitable Giving," NPR, August 20, 2012, http://www.npr.org/2012/08/20/158947667/study-reveals-the-geography-of-charitable-giving (accessed January 19, 2018).

36. Ken Stern, "Why the Rich Don't Give," *The Atlantic,* April 2013, https://www.theatlantic.com/magazine/archive/2013/04/why-the-rich-dont-give/309254/ (accessed January 19, 2018).

37. See "Reader's Digest Trust Poll: The 100 Most Trusted People in America (https://www.rd.com/culture/readers-digest-trust-poll-the-100-most-trusted-people-in-america/) and "Who Makes the List of Trustworthiness?" (http://www.npr.org/2015/02/14/386227424/who-makes-the-list-of-trustworthiness).

38. "What the Bible Says About Children, Poverty and Compassion," Compassion International, https://www.compassion.com/poverty/what-the-bible-says-children-poverty.htm (accessed January 19, 2018).

39. Michael Sanders and Francesca Tamma, "The Science Behind Why People Give Money to Charity," *The Guardian,* March 23, 2015, https://www.theguardian.com/voluntary-sector-network/2015/mar/23/the-science-behind-why-people-give-money-to-charity (accessed January 19, 2018).

40. Philip E. Tetlock, Orie V. Kristel, S. Beth Elson, Melanie C. Green and Jennifer S. Lerner, "The psychology of the unthinkable: Taboo trade-offs, forbidden base rates, and heretical counterfactuals," *Journal of Personality and Social Psychology* Volume 78.5, 2000, p. 853–870.

41. "SMART Goals: How to Make Your Goals Achievable," Mind Tools, https://www.mindtools.com/pages/article/smart-goals.htm (accessed January 19, 2018).

42. "The Millennium Development Goals Report 2015," United Nations, http://www.un.org/millenniumgoals/2015_MDG_Report/pdf/MDG%202015%20rev%20(July%201).pdf (accessed January 19, 2018).

43. "Poverty – United Nations Sustainable Development Goals," United Nations, http://www.un.org/sustainabledevelopment/poverty/ (accessed January 19, 2018).

44. S. Turkay, "Setting Goals: Who, Why, How?" manuscript, 2014, https://hilt.harvard.edu/files/hilt/files/settinggoals.pdf (accessed January 19, 2018).

45. Karen E. Jenni and George Loewenstein, "Explaining the "identifiable victim effect," *Journal of Risk and Uncertainty* Volume 14, 1997, p. 235–257.

46. Deborah A. Small and George Loewenstein, "Helping a Victim or Helping the Victim: Altruism and Identifiability," *Journal of Risk and Uncertainty* Volume 26, 2003, p. 5–16.

47. Deborah A. Small, George Loewenstein and Paul Slovic, "Can Insight Breed Callousness? The Impact of Learning about the Identifiable Victim Effect on Sympathy," Conference on Economics and Psychology, Toulouse, France, June 20–21, 2005.

48. Jennifer S. Lerner, Deborah A. Small and George Loewenstein, "Heart Strings and Purse Strings: Carryover Effects of Emotions on Economic Decisions," Psychological Science Volume 15.5, May 15, 2004, 9. 337–341.

49. Thomas C. Schelling, "The Life You Save May Be Your Own," in Samuel B. Chase ed. *Problems in Public Expenditure Analysis: Studies of Government Finance* (Washington: The Brookings Institution, 1968).

50. Derek D. Rucker and Richard E. Petty, "Emotion Specificity and Consumer Behavior: Anger, Sadness, and Preference for Activity," *Motivation and Emotion,* Volume 28.1, March 2004, p. 3–21.

51. Shane Frederick and George Loewenstein, "Hedonic Adaptation," in Daniel Kahneman, Edward Diener and Nortbert Schwarz, *Well-Being: Foundations of Hedonic Psychology* (New York, NY: Russell Sage Foundation, 2003).

52. *The State of Pastors* (Ventura, CA: Barna Group, 2017).

53. *The Generosity Gap.*

54. Jeffrey Brown, "World Bank Announces Goal to End Extreme Poverty by 2030," PBS, April 18, 2013, https://www.pbs.org/newshour/show/world-bank-announces-goal-to-end-extreme-poverty-by-2030 (accessed January 19, 2018).

55. Maria K. Pavlova and Rainer K. Silbereisen, "Dispositional optimism fosters opportunity-congruent coping with occupational uncertainty," *Journal of Personality* Volume 81.1, February 2013, p. 76–86.

56. Jaihyun Park and Mahzarin Banaji, "Mood and heuristics: The influence of happy and sad states on sensitivity and bias in stereotyping," *Journal of Personality and Social Psychology* Volume 78, July 2000, p. 1005–1023.

57. Lalin Anik, Lara B. Aknin, Michael I. Norton and Elizabeth W. Dunn, "Feeling Good About Giving: The Benefits (and Costs) of Self-Interested Charitable Behavior," Harvard Business School Marketing Unit Working Paper No. 10-012, August 6, 2009.

58. Stephen G. Post, "Altruism, happiness, and health: it's good to be good," *International Journal of Behavioral Medicine* Volume 12.2, June 2005, p. 66–77.

# GLOSSARY

## Generation

- *Millennials:* born between 1984 and 2002
- *Gen X:* born between 1965 and 1983
- *Boomers:* born between 1946 and 1964
- *Elders:* born between 1945 or earlier

## Ethnicity

Based on a multiple response question

- White / Caucasian
- Black / African American
- Hispanic / Latino
- Asian
- Other / more than one race and not defined in any of the above

## Region

- *Northeast* are residents of CT, DE, MA, MD, ME, NH, NJ, NY, PA, RI, VA, VT, WV, and Washington, DC
- *Midwest* are residents of IA, IL, IN, KS, KY, MI, MN, MO, ND, NE, OH, SD, and WI
- *South* are residents of AL, AR, FL, GA, LA, MS, NC, OK, SC, TN, and TX
- *West* are residents of AK, AZ, CA, CO, HI, ID, MT, NM, NV, OR, UT, WA, and WY

## Political Ideology

- *Conservatives:* identify as "mostly conservative" when it comes to political issues
- *Liberals:* identify as "mostly liberal" when it comes to political issues
- *Moderate:* identify as somewhere in between conservative and liberal

## Faith Identity

Respondents were asked to specify personal faith or affiliation.

- *Catholic:* self-identify as Catholic
- *Protestant:* self-identify as Protestant
- *Christian:* self-identify as Christian
- *Non-Christian:* do not self-identify as Christian
- *Other faith:* self-identify as faith other than Christianity
- *No faith:* self-identify as atheist, agnostic or no faith
- *Not sure:* were not able to choose any of the above categories

- *Practicing Christians* are self-identified Christians who say their faith is very important in their lives and have attended a worship service within the past month
- *Non-practicing Christians* are self-identified Christians who do not qualify as practicing.
- *Evangelical Christians* meet nine criteria, which include having made a personal commitment to Jesus Christ that is still important in their life today and believing that, when they die, they will go to heaven because they have confessed their sins and accepted Jesus Christ as their Savior. The seven other conditions include saying their faith is very important in their lives; believing they have a personal responsibility to share their religious beliefs about Christ with non-Christians; believing that Satan exists; believing that Jesus Christ lived a sinless life on earth; asserting that the Bible is accurate in all that it teaches; believing that eternal salvation is possible only through grace, not works; and describing God as the all-knowing, all-powerful, perfect deity who created the universe and still rules it today. Being classified as an evangelical is not dependent on church attendance or denominational affiliation, and respondents are not asked to describe themselves as "evangelical."

# METHODOLOGY

C

The data in this report originated from a series of research studies conducted by Barna Group of Ventura, California.

| Dates | Audience | Collection Method | Sample Size | Sample Error | Funded by |
|---|---|---|---|---|---|
| June 2003 | U.S. adults | Phone | 1,002 | ±2.9 | Compassion International |
| January 2005 and October 2005 | U.S. adults, aggregate data | Phone | 2,006 | ±2.0 | Barna |
| January 2008 | U.S. adults | Phone | 1,004 | ±2.9 | Barna |
| June 2008 | Protestant senior pastors | Telephone | 494 | ±4.5 | Compassion International |
| January 2011 | U.S. adults | Phone and online | 1,567 | ±2.3 | Barna |
| September 2011 | U.S. adults | Online | 1,429 | ±2.4 | Compassion International |
| January 2013 | U.S. adults | Phone and online | 2,036 | ±1.9 | Barna |
| December 2013 | U.S. adults | Online | 1,052 | ±2.9 | Compassion International |
| January 2015 | U.S. adults | Online | 806 | ±3.3 | Barna |
| April—May 2015 | U.S. adults | Online | 1,025 | ±2.9 | Pepperdine University |
| April 2016 | U.S. adults | Online | 1,097 | ±2.8 | Barna |

| June 2016 | Protestant senior pastors | Online | 606 | ±3.9 | Thrivent Financial |
| July–September 2016 | U.S. Christians | Online | 1,556 | ±2.3 | Thrivent Financial |
| May 2017 | U.S. adults | Online | 1,019 | ±2.9 | Barna |
| May 2017 | U.S. adults | Online | 1,001 | ±2.9 | Compassion International |
| May 2017 | Protestant senior pastors | Online | 609 | ±3.8 | Compassion International |

Protestant senior pastors, whether interviewed by phone or online, were recruited from publicly available church listings covering 90 percent of U.S. churches that have a physical address and a listed phone number or email address. Churches selected for inclusion were called up to five times at different times of the day to increase the probability of successful contact. Data were minimally weighted to match church characteristics from the National Congregation Study (by Association of Statisticians of American Religious Bodies) for denominational affiliation, church size and region.

Interviews with U.S. adults were conducted online and by telephone. All telephone interviews were conducted by Barna Group. All households were selected for inclusion in the sample using a random-digit dial technique, which allows every telephone household in the nation to have an equal and known probability of selection. Households selected for inclusion in the survey sample received multiple callbacks to increase the probability of obtaining a representative distribution of adults. Between 20 and 40 percent of telephone interviews were conducted on cell phones.

For pastor and U.S. adult surveys, regional quotas were used to ensure that sufficient population dispersion was achieved. There were also minimum and maximum ranges placed on the distribution of respondents within several demographic variables that were tracked during the field process to ensure that statistical weighting would not be excessive. When a particular attribute reached one of the parameters, the sampling selection process was varied to preclude individuals who did not meet the necessary demographic criterion, with the interviewer seeking a person from the same church or household who fit the desired criterion.

Online interviews were conducted using an online research panel based on probability sampling that covers both the online and offline populations in the U.S. The panel members are randomly recruited by telephone and by self-administered mail and web surveys. All potential panelists are randomly selected to join the panel; unselected volunteers are not able to join.

Once data was collected, minimal statistical weights were applied to several demographic variables to more closely correspond to known national averages. When researchers describe the accuracy of survey results, they usually provide the estimated amount of "sampling error." This refers to the degree of possible inaccuracy that could be attributed to interviewing a group of people that is not completely representative of the population from which they were drawn. See the table for maximum sampling error. There is a range of other errors that can influence survey results (e.g., biased question wording, question sequencing, inaccurate recording of responses, inaccurate data tabulation, etc.)—errors whose influence on the findings cannot be statistically estimated. Barna makes every effort to overcome these possible errors at every stage of research.

# ACKNOWLEDGMENTS D

Barna Group is incredibly grateful to Jimmy Mellado and Compassion International for their partnership on this study. Their commitment to excellence in the long-term and holistic development of children around the world is an example and a beacon, within the Church and beyond. We are especially thankful to Jerry Henderson, Jessica Engel, Ben Rough and Deb Krumland, whose collaboration made this project possible.

We appreciate the time and insights of our expert interviewees and contributors who bring this data to life and, more importantly, are heroes in the daily work of poverty alleviation: Mark Bowers, Dan Brewster, John Cortines, Emi Hernandez, Susan Mettes, Jessy Padilla and Michele Wymer.

The research for this study was coordinated by Brooke Hempell and Traci Hochmuth. Under the editorial direction of Roxanne Stone, the writing team includes Susan Mettes and Alyce Youngblood. Doug Brown proofread the manuscript. Chaz Russo designed the cover, and Annette Allen created the interior layout and data visualizations. Brenda Usery managed production.

Additional thanks for the support of our Barna colleagues: Amy Brands, Bill Denzel, Aly Hawkins, Pam Jacob, David Kinnaman, Steve McBeth, Elise Miller, Caitlin Schuman, Jess Villa and Todd White.

# ABOUT THE PROJECT PARTNERS

Barna Group is a research firm dedicated to providing actionable insights on faith and culture, with a particular focus on the Christian Church. Since 1984, Barna has conducted more than one million interviews in the course of hundreds of studies, and has become a go-to source for organizations that want to better understand a complex and changing world from a faith perspective.

Barna's clients and partners include a broad range of academic institutions, churches, nonprofits and businesses, such as Alpha, the Templeton Foundation, Fuller Seminary, the Bill and Melinda Gates Foundation, Maclellan Foundation, DreamWorks Animation, Focus Features, Habitat for Humanity, The Navigators, NBC-Universal, the ONE Campaign, Paramount Pictures, the Salvation Army, Walden Media, Sony and World Vision. The firm's studies are frequently quoted by major media outlets such as *The Economist*, BBC, CNN, *USA Today,* the *Wall Street Journal*, Fox News, Huffington Post, *The New York Times* and the *Los Angeles Times*.

Compassion International is a child-advocacy ministry that pairs compassionate people with those who are suffering from poverty "to release children from poverty in Jesus' name." Through physical, social, economic and spiritual care, they help children fully mature in every facet of life and transcend a legacy of poverty. Compassion partners with indigenous local churches to address the holistic, long-term needs of children of all faiths, cultures, backgrounds and races. Their child sponsorship program is the only one validated as effective through independent, empirical research. With nearly 7,000 international church partners in Asia, Africa, South America, Central America and the Caribbean, Compassion has sponsored more than 1.8 million children over the past 65 years.

 www.Barna.com

 www.Compassion.com

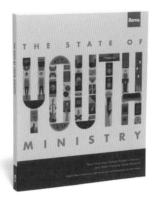

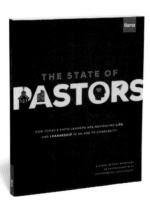

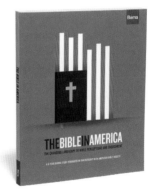